# CONRAIL

**TIMOTHY SCOTT DOHERTY & BRIAN SOLOMON**

MBI

# DEDICATION

*This book is dedicated to Tim's wife, Dawn.*

*On the front cover:* On a July afternoon in 1998, four of Conrail's SD80MACs move the westbound FRSE (Framingham to Selkirk) over the Boston Line.

*On the frontispiece:* Eastward Conrail ASIN-1(Alton & Southern/St. Louis to Indianapolis) uses track No. 2 at Haley Tower in Terre Haute, Indiana. This tower controlled the junction of Conrail's St. Louis Line with CSX's Chicago–Evansville, the former Chicago & Eastern Illinois mainline. *Peter Ruesch*

*On the title page:* The eastward RRT-12 rolls through Rochester, New York, on June 8, 1983. Conrail's U36Bs were built for Auto Train, but were sold to Conrail as its first new locomotives. *Doug Eisele*

*On the back cover:* Conrail's Office Car Special made a rare appearance on the Corning Secondary at Himrod Junction, New York, on September 1, 1987. The former New York Central line crossed over the former PRR Elmira Branch at Himrod.

The first day that CSX and Norfolk Southern could exercise control over Conrail, which they had jointly purchased, was August 22, 1998. Until then, they were barred from exerting control over Conrail operations. On that evening, Conrail's SEAL (Selkirk to Allentown) rolls across Iona Island on the River Line.

Edited by Amy Glaser
Designed by LeAnn Kuhlmann

Printed in China

## *Acknowledgements*

Numerous people helped us in our travels and research. Brian's father, Richard Jay Solomon, introduced him to Conrail's predecessors at a formative age. Richard lent his vast library of books, maps, timetables and photographs. Our friend Pat Yough helped in many ways and authored the section on the Monongahela. Doug Eisele was very generous with his photography, help with proofreading the Albany Division, and lent expertise on many subjects. Robert A. Buck introduced the authors to each other, and many years earlier, introduced Brian to Washington Hill. The Hoover family lent experience and companionship in maters regarding locomotives and the PRR. Thanks to Otto for his artwork and enthusiasm for Rochester, New York.

Tim's father, Robert J. Doherty, took him on Sunday morning trips to explore Penn Central's and Conrail's operations around Rochester, New York. Victor Stone shared the correct method for following Conrail's Office Car Special, and later provided many schedules of the train as it ended runs around the system in high style. Tom Mangan, Fred Shaffer, and Gordon Smith introduced Tim to Washington Hill and the River Line. Charles Tipton's daily emails of trains running over Conaumge line made for interesting reading each morning during 1997. The New Jersey Turnpike Authority was gracious enough to provide a large enough shoulder on the Newark Bay Extension.

The Cornell University Library System was very helpful in providing many of the sources used for the history portion of the book. The Washington Post's extensive online archive of stories, particularly those written by Don Phillips, was very useful in understanding the political nature Conrail existence. The January 1998 Transportation Research Board panel discussion on Conrail, especially the James Blaze presentation, was instrumental in helping Conrail's place railroad history.

Several photographers were generous and lent images included here. Each is credited for their material. In addition, we have traveled with many photographers over the years and would like to thank all for their input and help.

Lastly we thank all the employees of Conrail who made the railroad what it was. Thanks for the tours, the insight, the visits, and the cab rides!

—*Tim Doherty and Brian Solomon*

# CONTENTS

# INTRODUCTION

*Right:* On April 1, 1976, Conrail was created. Conrail trimmed the Northeast railroad network and gradually restored the industry's profitability. General Electric B23-7 1976 was one of many new locomotives purchased by Conrail in its early years. *Brian Solomon*

*Inset:* Both authors have Rochester, New York, in common. Tim grew up there when his father was the director of the International Museum of Photography at George Eastman House, and Brian earned a Bachelor of Fine Arts in photographic illustration at the Rochester Institute of Technology. Both enjoyed watching Conrail operations here and around the system. *Brian Solomon*

Its prime arteries pulsing with traffic, Conrail appeared to have an incongruous duality. On the Water Level Route west of Buffalo, or the former PRR Middle Division, Conrail provided a never-ending parade of mainline freight. It seemed all you needed was to snap your fingers, and a headlight would appear and three six-motor diesels with a hundred or more cars in tow would roar past you. Late-era Conrail rights of way were well maintained with deep ballast and heavy rail, but the dark side to Conrail's persona was ever present. The company was constantly shrinking, and the ruins of its shed lines were evident at every turn. Endless reports of line and yard closures, sales, abandonments, mainline rationalizations, and tower razings made it seem like Conrail would eventually self-destruct.

If Conrail had failed, American railroading might have failed with it, and freight railroads would not be enjoying relative prosperity today. But Conrail was formed to disappear and was never intended to last indefinitely. Conrail's ultimate demise, its split between Norfolk Southern and CSX, was a function of its success, not its failure. From this, Conrail will be remembered as a success.

This book is neither comprehensive nor exhaustive, but we do hope to enlighten you about Conrail's origins, struggles, and successes.

—*Brian Solomon and Tim Doherty*

# CHAPTER ONE

# PRELUDE TO CONRAIL

## *Descent in to the Maelstrom*

By the 1950s, railroads in the industrialized eastern United States suffered from decline. Highway competition had started to erode their supremacy in the 1920s. Branch lines, small freight shipments, and light passenger services were the first to be attacked. Railroads weathered the Great Depression and experienced a traffic boom during World War II, but faced more intensive competition from highway traffic and other modes of transportation in the postwar years. Construction of the federally sponsored interstate highway system accelerated in the 1960s, and other highway projects allowed trucks to compete more effectively with railroads for the most lucrative traffic. Competition, combined with industrial decline and a shift away from coal traffic, further eroded railroad profits.

Penn Central westward intermodal train TV 5 rolls through Buffalo on January 26, 1973. Penn Central was born from the hope that a merger between the nation's two largest railroads, money would be saved by reduced operating costs and the elimination of duplicative routes. Poor premerger preparation resulted in operational chaos, and excessive government regulation limited opportunities to reduce trackage and cut costs. Penn Central floundered into bankruptcy within two years. *Doug Eisele*

The situation was especially acute in the Northeast, where demographic and economic changes forced many businesses to move south and west. Traditional railroad-based industries were among the first to go. Railroads faced a host of serious problems, such as growing passenger deficits; loss of the most profitable freight; archaic, inflexible labor agreements that resulted in low productivity and high costs; strict federal rate regulations; duplicate route structures; and high terminal costs.

Initially, the postwar economic boom veiled the problems facing the railroad industry. Prosperity allowed railroads to improve their rolling stock and locomotives. Centralized traffic control (CTC) was implemented to allow direct remote control of switches and signals and permitted one person to do many jobs. Computerized hump yards were built to consolidate smaller yards and reduce terminal costs. Many lines,

including New York Central and New Haven, made moves toward intermodal transport and introduced piggyback services to more effectively compete with trucking.

## MERGER MACHINATIONS

Since the 1920s, railroaders, pundits, and politicians had talked of mass mergers that would join the many traditional companies into a few large regional systems. In the late 1950s, this concept found renewed interest. One of the most prominent schemes was proposed by newly appointed Pennsylvania Railroad (PRR) President James Symes, who wanted to merge PRR with its longtime rival, New York Central (NYC). Symes believed that cost savings from combining the two companies' duplicate networks would revitalize the railroads.

Symes' vision to join the nation's two largest railroads was premature and alarmed the industry. Pennsy and Central had always

Pennsylvania Railroad's Horseshoe Curve is seen here on a summer afternoon in 1963 from the rocks below Kittanning Point. An eastbound freight descends on the No. 2 track. Eighteen years later, in March 1981, Conrail rationalized this mainline and lifted the number two track. *Richard Jay Solomon*

vied for traffic, and their megamerger seemed to violate traditional empire-building logic. New York Central's president, Alfred Perlman, spurned PRR's proposal. He believed NYC was better suited to join a proposed Baltimore & Ohio (B&O)/Chesapeake & Ohio (C&O) combination. The financially stronger C&O rejected Perlman's proposal.

In 1961, the top executives of C&O, B&O, and PRR held a railroad summit in the heart of C&O country at White Sulphur Springs, West Virginia, and essentially redrew the map of eastern railroading and set the stage for the big mergers of the 1960s. They agreed that the most desirable combinations would be B&O/C&O plus PRR/NYC, and Norfolk & Western (N&W) plus Wabash and Nickel Plate. To make this happen, PRR gave up significant holdings in the N&W (35 percent) and Wabash (87 percent). Control of these lines had long provided PRR with significant dividends. With NYC finances deteriorating, Perlman

acquiesced to PRR's plans and merger negotiations began.

### ERIE LACKAWANNA
Prior to the big NYC/PRR consolidation, Erie and Lackawanna executives were among

New York Central was the second largest passenger carrier in the United States. In February 1949, Electro-Motive F3s lead train 27, the westward *New England States Limited* on the Boston & Albany in Framingham, Massachusetts. *George C. Corey*

New Alco FAs were posed for publicity near the Meadville, Pennsylvania, Yard in March 1948. Although it was the weakest New York–Chicago trunk line, after World War II, Erie Railroad made large capital investments and was the first trunk line to haul 100 percent of its freight by diesels. *Erie Railroad Photograph, Tim Doherty collection*

Shortly after the Erie Lackawanna merger in 1960, a Lackawanna-painted E8A leads a passenger train near Dearborn Station in Chicago. Although Erie Lackawanna intended to save its component railroads from financial oblivion, it only postponed the line's incurable insolvency. Bankrupt and spurned by Norfolk & Western and Chessie System, EL was forced to join Conrail in 1976. *Richard Jay Solomon*

This westward mail train carrying Flexivan containers around Horseshoe Curve illustrates one of Pennsylvania and New York Central's numerous inconsistent operating philosophies. Pennsylvania Railroad was a founder of the Trailer Train equipment pool that promoted intermodal trailers riding on railroad flatcars. In contrast, New York Central promoted its specialized Flexivan containers system. In the end, Conrail adopted PRR's equipment approach and New York Central's intermodal train symbol system. *Doug Eisele*

A quintet of New Haven Alco FA diesels lead a freight on Maybrook Line. This once-important gateway withered after Penn Central assumed control of New Haven in 1969. Traffic was diverted to other routes. The eastern portion of the Maybrook Line from Hopewell Junction to Devon had a minor revival in the late 1980s and early 1990s when Conrail routed its SENH/NHSE (Selkirk to New Haven) trains over the line. *Richard Jay Solomon*

the first to enter serious merger discussions in 1954. The two railroads' double-track mainlines ran parallel to Buffalo and were nearly adjacent for miles across the Southern Tier of New York. Erie was fearful that Lackawanna would merge with the Nickel Plate to create an aggressive, new, single carrier between the Port of New York and Chicago. Lackawanna existed in the dark shadow of its coal-hauling past and needed help to survive. Initially a three-way merger with Delaware & Hudson (D&H) was discussed, but D&H was financially better off and remained independent.

The Erie Lackawanna (EL) merger was approved by the Interstate Commerce Commission (ICC) on September 13, 1960, and became effective on October 17. Traffic was funneled into the best of the combined route structure to allow some lines to be downgraded and abandoned, notably Lackawanna's mainline west of Binghamton. This gave some

relief to the combined company's problems, but the larger issues of passenger losses, declining traffic, and high labor costs continued to plague EL. By 1963, the railroad was on the brink of collapse, but financial doom was forestalled when the board of directors brought in William White to run the railroad.

## PENN CENTRAL

The Penn Central (PC) merger forged ahead through the mid-1960s. After setting the wheels of the PC merger in motion, James Symes retired in 1963 and left his handpicked successor, Stuart Saunders, formerly of N&W, to implement his proposed Penn Central merger. Despite his great experience, Saunders' merger preparations were flawed.

One obstacle to the PC merger was organized labor. Since consolidations and line reductions were major merger goals, labor leaders recognized that jobs were at stake. To gain needed labor support, Penn Central planners agreed to significant labor protection. This protection seriously impaired the new company's ability to trim its labor force, so the newborn Penn Central agreed to employ more people than needed. Labor agreements were complex, and the World War I-era work rules that remained in place obviated many efficiencies theoretically gained by a modern merged railroad.

One of Penn Central's most obvious failings was its management structure. The former competitors needed to work together as one team instead of fighting with each other.

Soon after the merger, disaster struck. Misrouted freight cars and misdirected trains caused havoc. PC's operational problems were complex and eluded rapid solutions. Breakdowns in billing and car control made it difficult to bill for service provided. Historian Stephen Salisbury, in his exhaustive study of Penn Central, maintains that the service and operational meltdown was directly responsible for its bankruptcy less than two years after the merger was consummated. Poor service forced customers to seek

New York Central operated two parallel lines west of Albany. The Water Level Route and its West Shore subsidiary and connections between the two lines provided operational flexibility. On May 4, 1974, a quartet of Penn Central F7s lead a train onto the West Shore at Wayneport, New York. This section between Wayneport and Fairport was later abandoned, although Fairport to Chili Junction was retained as a bypass around Rochester, New York. *R.R. Richardson, Doug Eisele collection*

Erie Lackawanna reassigned E-units to through freight services after they were bumped from passenger duties. Erie Lackawanna E8A 817 leads a freight through the scenic Canisteo Valley near Cameron, New York, on January 21, 1973. *Doug Eisele*

other solutions by shifting traffic to other railroads and trucks, which cost the railroad traffic and revenue.

## MOUNTAINS OF DEBT

On the eve of the merger, Penn Central borrowed a huge sum of money to pay for new equipment, track renewal, and modernization efforts needed to implement the merger. Big spending continued once the merger was complete, and as PC's losses mounted, it incurred additional debt. With revenues in freefall, PC was unable to make its loan payments. PC's damaged credit precluded additional loans and investment, and its operating losses in the first three months of 1970 were more than railroad executives had expected for the entire year. When its last-ditch request for a loan from the federal

government was denied, the railroad filed for bankruptcy.

## ERIE LACKAWANNA DOOMED

In response to the proposed Penn Central merger, Erie Lackawanna wanted to be included in the Norfolk & Western–Nickel Plate–Wabash merger of 1964. The ICC agreed and required N&W to support EL as a condition of the merger.

In 1965, Norfolk & Western and the combined C&O/B&O plotted a defensive merger strategy in response to PC. Under intense pressure from the ICC, N&W considered merging smaller eastern roads, including EL, D&H, Reading, and Central Railroad of New Jersey, to form a strong competitor to Penn Central. Ultimately, only Erie Lackawanna and Delaware & Hudson

Three Lehigh Valley Alco C-420s lead eastward freight SJ-4 near Athens, Pennsylvania, on October 5, 1974. Lehigh Valley was one of several northeastern railroads that maintained its loyalty to Alco through the 1960s. It ordered Alco's 2,000 horsepower four-motor C-420s and 2,750 horsepower six-motor C-628s. Most of Lehigh Valley's C-420s were transferred to Delaware & Hudson when Conrail took over LV in 1976. *Doug Eisele*

were included. N&W was not pleased and protested, but the ICC, with support of the Supreme Court, coerced N&W into supporting both EL and D&H. N&W had concerns about EL's high debt and poor finances, and created a holding company, called Dereco, to shield it from EL's and D&H's financial liabilities. N&W assumed control of EL in April 1968, and made it a wholly owned subsidiary, but EL retained its identity. Incidentally, despite early intentions, the anticipated merger of Norfolk & Western and C&O never materialized.

Norfolk & Western's control secured EL's westward connections at Buffalo. N&W and EL jointly built Bison Yard—a modern classification yard—on the site of Lackawanna's old East Buffalo facility. N&W brought new business to EL and provided dedicated run-through trains over the Nickel Plate Routes that connected New York and St. Louis. In September 1970, EL introduced a dedicated intermodal train for United Parcel Service (UPS).

Despite N&W efforts to boost EL, the line remained financially weak. Fundamental cost and rate problems and the continued

erosion of EL's traditional traffic base were unchecked by N&W support. The most prominent example on EL was the Maybrook gateway with former New Haven. This once-major Erie interchange point was effectively torpedoed by PC, which was reported to have deliberately provided poor service. By 1971, traffic had been reduced to a trickle of cars despite bitter protests from EL to the ICC.

EL turned a profit in 1969, but lost money in 1970 and 1971, and the bottom fell out of the weak EL in 1972. In June of that year, Hurricane Agnes sent a deluge across the southern tier of New York that caused more than $40 million in damage to the railroads. Erie Lackawanna suffered roughly 200 miles of washouts on its mainlines. The important section between Owego and Salamanca, New York, was hit the hardest. In the wake of the storm damage, Norfolk & Western had their Erie Lackawanna subsidiary seek bankruptcy protection.

## KILLED BY THE CURE?

Instead of sorting out the railroads' fundamental problems, mergers exacerbated an already difficult situation. Penn Central was

the worst case, but most northeastern carriers were also in deep trouble. In the wake of Penn Central's financial collapse, Lehigh Valley (LV) entered bankruptcy just days after PC.

Jersey Central (CNJ), LV's longtime competitor, was in worse shape and had been bankrupt since 1967. Traditionally, one-third of CNJ's routes served eastern Pennsylvania. The railroad had once been a significant anthracite carrier, but as this traffic dried up, CNJ was stuck with a network of vastly under-utilized freight trackage. To address this problem, CNJ and Lehigh Valley consolidated their lines between Wilkes-Barre and Allentown in 1965 to form a more efficient route and abandon unneeded track. This did little to help CNJ, and its fortunes continued to spiral downward. In 1971, CNJ pulled out of Pennsylvania entirely, including routes it had picked up from the defunct Lehigh & New England less than 10 years earlier, which reduced its total route mileage to just 402.

To help address its passenger problems, New Jersey funded the Aldene Plan line-relocation project in 1967, which shifted commuter trains to Newark's Penn Station over a short section of the Lehigh Valley between Aldene and Hunter Tower in Newark, and from there, over the former PRR. This allowed CNJ to close its Jersey City terminal and ferry connection to New York City, and provide a more convenient commuter transfer to midtown Manhattan via the Penn tunnels.

Reading Company, which made its fortunes moving anthracite coal and Philadelphia's suburban traffic, was another troubled line. The availability of cheap foreign oil combined with stifling coal strikes in the late 1940s hastened a widespread switch to oil for heating, which dramatically reduced demand for the Reading's coal.

Baltimore & Ohio had maintained control of the Reading since 1886 and allowed B&O access to the New York area through the Reading's controlling interest in the Central Railroad of New Jersey. The

Eastern railroads shared many common problems such as unprofitable suburban commuter services. Central Railroad of New Jersey suffered more than others because it supported an extensive commuter network and maintained a complex of urban freight terminals, but it only profited from unusually short mainline hauls. It was the first Conrail predecessor to sink into financial abyss. CNJ GP7 1524 was photographed in Elizabeth, New Jersey. *Patrick Yough collection*

17

New Haven's former Virginian EF-4 rectifier electrics 304 and 302 lead a freight near Pelham Bay Park. As late as 1955, 18 daily freights were scheduled to operate in each direction west of Cedar Hill. The death knell for New Haven's freight empire was the construction of Interstate 95 between New York and Boston in 1956. This multilane freeway paralleled the railroad's entire mainline. It was much faster to drive loads across the Hudson than to use the circuitous Maybrook Gateway or the slow freight ferries. Within a decade, most of New Haven's remaining freight had taken to the roads. *Tim Doherty collection*

Reading and CNJ, along with the B&O, provided one of the four direct routes between New York and Chicago.

At its peak, Reading Terminal in Philadelphia accommodated roughly 18,000 passengers daily and was served by 450 to 500 daily passenger trains. In 1929, Reading began to electrify its suburban lines with an 11-kilo-volt, 25-hertz overhead system, the same as the PRR and New Haven.

In 1958, Philadelphia was among the first cities in the United States to provide a public subsidy to cover operational losses through its Passenger Service Improvement Corporation (PSIC). The South Eastern Pennsylvania Transportation Authority (SEPTA) was created in 1962, and organized fares, policies, and subsidies to Reading Company and PRR rail commuter operations by 1968.

For a while it looked as if Reading would fall under the umbrella of C&O/B&O. Penn Central's difficulties grew, and combined with concerns of Reading's mounting losses and suburban passenger obligations, C&O/B&O

soured toward the merger. The companies did not include Reading in their system plan. In 1971, the B&O sold its 35 percent interest in Reading at a loss, which forced Reading to seek bankruptcy protection.

## ON THE BRINK OF OBLIVION

It appeared as if all of eastern railroading was on the brink of oblivion. By 1973, 13 percent of the nation's track miles were owned by railroads in bankruptcy, and the severity of this situation threatened the nation's economy. Washington policymakers had to provide relief to ailing northeastern railroads or face a total collapse of railroad transport. This set in motion the process of deregulation, which gradually reformed the entire American railroad industry.

## GOVERNMENT BAILOUT?

In the mid-1970s, American railroads started to accept large subsidies to cover passenger and freight losses. In order for the industry to survive and prosper again, drastic government action was needed.

In June 1972, Hurricane Agnes brought heavy rain to New York and Pennsylvania. Widespread flooding washed out tracks and damaged bridges. Although Erie Lackawanna was hit the hardest, Lehigh Valley also suffered damage, which is evidenced by this bridge in Athens, Pennsylvania, where flooding damaged one of the bridge piers. On January 21, 1973, three Alco C420s led by Lehigh Valley 405 are about to bring westward freight JB-3 across the damaged bridge. *Doug Eisele*

A former Cleveland Union Terminal P-motor leads Penn Central passenger train near Tarrytown. New York Central's intensive New York suburban network was once heralded as one of the finest operations in modern railroading. *Tim Doherty collection*

Failed public policy in the form of rigid government rate regulation, complex and expensive abandonment procedures, and support for inefficient labor practices had put railroads in a bind. During the 1950s and 1960s, in the face of declining traffic, increased competition from other modes of transportation, and rising costs, railroads couldn't effectively lower costs by cutting tracks, obtaining more efficient labor agreements, or raising prices. Bankruptcy was the only solution.

In 1887, Congress created the Interstate Commerce Commission (ICC), the nation's first federal regulatory agency. Through a series of congressional acts over the years, the ICC gained significant power to regulate railroads. It set minimum and maximum rates for hauling freight and passengers, determined safety standards, and oversaw route changes and abandonments. In order to change rates, railroads had to justify increases or decreases to the ICC through expensive and complicated proceedings.

Railroad labor laws enacted in the 1910s and 1920s had limited the companies' ability to alter labor arrangements. This made it difficult for railroads to tailor labor arrangements to take best advantage of new labor-saving technology years later.

The 1920 Transportation Act had given the ICC broad powers over track abandonments, extensions, and mergers. Railroads, unlike other businesses, were under legal obligation to provide public service and could not discontinue service without ICC approval. Regulations tended to favor shippers. The ICC often mandated that railroads retain unprofitable operations, while rate regulation prevented railroads from raising rates to sufficiently cover costs.

Line abandonment was a slow, difficult, and expensive process. While the ICC granted many abandonment applications, it did not have a consistent abandonment policy and reviewed each application on a case-by-case basis. A U.S. Department of Transportation report to Congress in 1973 blasted ICC's "patchwork policy that had maintained essentially the same railroad network, which was in place in 1920, one which was geared to the environment and economy of the late nineteenth and early twentieth century."

Passenger services were the first to suffer from highway competition. During the 1930s, intercity passenger services were hit hard, but they rebounded during World War II when fuel and vehicle rationing, combined with an unusually high demand for travel, encouraged rail ridership. After the war, widespread car ownership, intensive state and federally sponsored road building and improvements—culminating in the construction of the interstate highway system in the 1960s—and the growth of the domestic airline industry contributed to the drastic loss of railroad ridership.

In the wake of the Penn Central financial meltdown, Congress created the National Railroad Passenger Corporation (Amtrak) in 1971 to relieve PC and other privately operated railroads of their long-distance passenger responsibilities.

## INFRASTRUCTURE OR BUSINESS?

Despite the predominant worldwide view of railways as public infrastructure, American railroads were always thought of as private enterprises and were expected to earn a profit. By the 1970s, when eastern railroads had slid into the abyss of bankruptcy, many feared that this signaled the insolvency of the entire industry.

## CALL TO ACTION

On February 8, 1973, a one-day strike shut down Penn Central. This event forced Congress to take action. Despite Penn Central's poor performance and dire financial situation, the railroad was still integral to the nation's economy. It was feared that the results of a total Penn Central shutdown and liquidation would affect nearly half the manufacturing plants in the nation, and cause an estimated 2.7 percent decline in the gross national product within two months of service cessation.

Congress authorized stopgap grants to cover the railroad's short-term financial losses and keep PC running until the economy improved. Bankruptcy trustees appointed to sort out Penn Central's finances reported that the company was incapable of reorganizing under the traditional bankruptcy process, and liquidation was considered.

Labor leaders and members of Congress called for the nationalization of the entire American railroad network. One compromise

With in months of its formation, Penn Central was in ruins. The company logo was a symbolized 'P' and 'C' intertwined to represent the union of Pennsylvania Railroad and New York Central. This rust-stained logo on a PC box car sums up the sad state of the railroad. *Brian Solomon*

proposal was to create a firewall to isolate and nationalize terminal lines in the Northeast to protect long-haul carriers. The U.S. Department of Transportation rejected nationalization as an expensive and unnecessary exercise unlikely to produce the most efficient rail transportation system.

In response to outright nationalization, Union Pacific President Frank Barnett proposed an alternative to railroad nationalization that led to the federally-sponsored Conrail. Barnett proposed this concept to Dick Shoup, junior republican congressman from Montana—a rural state that depended on a vibrant national railroad system to transport its goods. Shoup sought Barnett's advice because he was concerned that Congress was not addressing the difficult problems of the railroad crisis in the Northeast.

Barnett conceived a federally created, public-private corporation that would organize a financially viable core network from the ruins of bankrupt railroads, and provide public financing until the new railroad could become self sustaining. This was based on models established by existing public-private corporations such as Federal National Mortgage Association (Fannie Mae) and Amtrak.

As the Barnett and Shoup proposal moved through Congress, it became the Regional Rail Reorganization (3-R) Act and

set planning for Conrail in motion. The 3-R Act was passed by Congress in December 1973, and was signed by President Nixon on January 2, 1974. The 3-R Act was unprecedented legislation that empowered the federal government to seize assets of the bankrupt railroads and reorganize them into a for-profit corporation wholly owned by the government. To plan, create, and later fund the new railroad, the act established the United States Railway Association (USRA), a nonprofit corporation with its directors appointed by the president. (The USRA is not to be confused with the United States Railroad Administration.) The new railroad was named the Consolidated Rail Corporation, Conrail for short.

The USRA was born in haste and faced conflicting tasks. Its primary objective was to create a financially self-sustaining railroad from the ruins of the bankrupt lines. It also had to maintain competition with other modes of transportation and rail carriers, and allow Conrail to regain traffic lost during its bankruptcy period. In addition, the USRA facilitated the development of the

Northeast Corridor as a high-speed passenger route. One of the USRA's responsibilities was to minimize the negative effects of line abandonment on railroad employees and local communities.

These conflicting goals made the USRA's policy decisions difficult. The USRA needed to weigh concerns of railroad labor, line-side communities, and shippers against a viable economic plan that would create a profit for Conrail. Another difficulty the USRA faced was short deadlines. A Conrail plan was needed quickly, and the USRA needed to act fast.

The 3-R Act gave judges of bankrupt railroads 120 days to determine if failed railroads would be able to undertake a traditional reorganization or if they should be included in Conrail. Conrail planners faced objections from trustees of bankrupt railroads who challenged the 3-R Act. They claimed that seizing private property was unconstitutional. The Supreme Court rejected these arguments and allowed the USRA to move forward and plan for Conrail.

Reading's Rutherford, Pennsylvania, yards were its primary facilities in the Harrisburg area. Although Reading's Harrisburg–Reading mainline became a primary Conrail freight corridor, its Rutherford Yard was not part of Conrail's longterm freight plans. Conrail saved a lot by closing and consolidating facilities inherited from predecessor roads. *J.C. Smith Jr., Patrick Yough Collection*

As Congress and the USRA worked out a solution, the northeastern railroad crisis continued to worsen. In November 1974, PC's net losses were more than twice those in 1973 (taking into account an 18 percent increase in freight rates). Its traffic was spiraling downward, and in December 1974, PC reported its lowest car loadings since the merger. The March 1975 issue of *TRAINS Magazine* reported that PC struggled along with only the help of government loans to cover losses—then approaching $1 million a day.

The 3-R Act required the USRA to develop a preliminary system plan and present it to the ICC. This preliminary plan had proposed a three-railroad Conrail solution. Under this plan, Conrail would be created from Penn Central and portions of smaller insolvent railroads. Competition would be provided by Norfolk & Western and/or Chessie System (C&O/B&O), which obtained new routes from Reading and Jersey Central trackage in New York, Pennsylvania, and New Jersey. The retention of 3,400 miles of light-density lines out of the 9,600 miles studied for possible abandonment was recommended.

In addition to this favored preliminary plan, the USRA had also reviewed a number of alternative Conrail system plans. These included blending all the bankrupt railroads into one gigantic unified Conrail system; the creation of two new railroads, one to serve as an eastern terminal carrier beyond the Firewall and the other as the long-distance carrier to western connections; the creation of two competing Conrail systems by splitting PC into roughly its PRR and NYC components; and organizing Conrail with a neutral terminal company that has access to key facilities and other railroads through extensive trackage rights.

Of these four alternative plans, the first choice, of a single, all-encompassing Conrail, was thought to be the best model for a self-sustaining, financially viable railroad. However, this plan was not immediately endorsed because it could create a Conrail monopoly in numerous key markets. Yet this plan attracted favor because the other alternative plans were too costly to implement and less efficient to operate.

## ERIE LACKAWANNA JOINS CONRAIL

Before the USRA preliminary system plan was released, Erie Lackawanna complicated issues for USRA planners. Initially, EL didn't want to be included in Conrail. EL's executives and bankruptcy trustees believed it was better for the railroad to reorganize under traditional means. On January 9, 1975, they changed their minds as it became clear that the railroad would not be able to survive on its own. The courts decided that EL could join the 3-R Act process, and the USRA planners would then consider how EL would fit into its final system plan (FSP).

After obtaining input on the preliminary plans and incorporating the Erie Lackawanna, the USRA drafted its FSP, which featured a modified three-railroad solution.

The FSP envisioned a Conrail system created from bankrupt lines—with a variety of key routes from the bankrupt lines sold to Chessie System and Southern Railway—to ensure competition with the government-created railroad. Under the FSP arrangement, Conrail would have primarily consisted of Penn Central routes plus selected portions of smaller railroads such as the Lehigh Valley. The

Chessie System would have taken many of the Erie Lackawanna, Central New Jersey, and Reading routes, which meshed nicely with Chessie's existing lines; while Southern would have assumed operation of Penn Central lines on the Delmarva Peninsula. Amtrak was selected to operate the Northeast Corridor as a high-speed passenger route. The USRA's initial Conrail plan was developed in just 23 months, beginning with the passage of the 3-R Act in December 1973 and ending with the approval of FSP by Congress on November 9, 1975.

## FINAL SYSTEM PLAN NOT FINAL

Although USRA's FSP was deemed the most palatable Conrail solution, it could not be implemented. The 3-R Act required labor unions and new railroads to agree on changes to work rules before the transfer of lines could take place. As described by H. Roger Grant in *Erie Lackawanna: The Death of an American Railroad, 1938–1992*, the labor agreements proved to be a crucial stumbling block in negotiations with solvent carriers. Neither the Chessie System nor Southern would agree to 3-R Act labor protection conditions. They had reservations about assuming operation of bankrupt lines because, unlike Conrail, they would not receive federal assistance to cover the costs of the labor agreements. The financial risks seemed to outweigh the advantages.

The Chessie System and Southern backed out, so the USRA was left with little choice but to fall back on its preferred alternative to its FSP and create a single, large Conrail system. In this rushed solution, the USRA faced objections over the lack of rail competition. It responded to these objections by granting trackage rights to Delaware & Hudson over certain Conrail Lines, allowing it to reach markets and gateways in eastern Pennsylvania; New Jersey; Alexandria, Virginia; and western New York.

Despite working under tight deadlines, facing conflicting goals, and receiving mixed support from the Nixon administration, USRA planners had created a framework for Conrail.

Lehigh Valley Apollo-1 intermodal train was photographed in Buffalo on January 26, 1973. The Apollo intermodal trains were jointly run by LV and N&W. After Conrail assumed operations on LV, Delaware & Hudson was responsible for the Apollo runs. An expanded D&H that ran via trackage rights over select Conrail lines was a last minute USRA option to provide competition to Conrail. *Doug Eisele*

25

## CHAPTER TWO

# OUT OF THE WOODS AND INTO THE BLUE

Conrail was born on April 1, 1976. On day one, Conrail was the largest railroad in the United States. According to Conrail's 1976 annual report, it encompassed more than 34,000 track miles and represented roughly 17,000 route miles that spanned from Boston to St. Louis and from Quebec to Washington, D.C. On its roster were more than 4,900 locomotives and 152,000 freight cars. It employed roughly 96,000 employees and moved more than 1,500 freight trains and 1,864 daily commuter trains transporting 360,000 passengers.

In its earliest days, Conrail was a unified railroad in name alone. Locomotives still carried the liveries of Penn Central, Erie Lackawanna, and Lehigh Valley. Gradually, equipment was renumbered and lettered for Conrail. A wash of blue paint was to follow, but eight years into Conrail, predecessor liveries could still be seen on locomotives. Signs reading New York Central can still

In April 1978, a westward freight climbs west through Bennington Curve near the summit of the Alleghenies on Conrail's Pittsburgh Line. One of Conrail's former EL SDP45s is leading. Tie piles along the right of way indicate the federally funded reconstruction of Conrail's lines is underway. *George S. Pitarys*

Conrail paint couldn't gloss over the heritage of its predecessors. *Brian Solomon*

*Right:* Its April 29, 1976, and Conrail is 29 days old. Former Erie Lackawanna GP35s work on the former New York Central at Cleveland. Conrail shifted traffic off EL lines west of Youngstown in favor of the former Penn Central routes. Although this train is following a Penn Central routing, it is probably carrying traffic that was moved by Erie Lackawanna a month earlier. *Bill Dechau, Doug Eisele collection*

contemporary operations. Line reductions were made to compensate for inherited redundancies and eliminate the poorest-performing branchlines.

Conrail's managers immediately came to the troubling realization that the railroad was in much worse shape than revealed in the USRA studies. The track suffered from deferred maintenance, and its locomotive fleet was tired and in desperate need of overhaul. The USRA plan anticipated a significant effort to restore and rehabilitate Conrail's physical plant. These efforts focused on rebuilding mainlines and removing slow orders. Improving track conditions was a key strategy in restoring freight services to acceptable levels.

In its earliest days, Conrail's line was plagued with hundreds of miles of mainline slow orders that increased transit times between yards. Edward Jordan remarked in *Inside Track* that, "we had 10-mile-an-hour slow orders all over the railroad, we couldn't

be found. It took years for Conrail to establish its own distinctive identity, and even until the last days of its operation, elements of its predecessors' character rippled just below the surface of the Conrail Blue.

Conrail's first chairman was Edward Jordan, who had previously led the USRA. Jordan was an outsider, chosen by the USRA specifically because he had no close ties with the railroad industry. It was hoped he would be free from the bias and culture believed to be part of the railroading crisis in the Northeast.

Jordan's management attempted to avoid the ill effects of the Penn Central fiasco and overcome the operational inefficiencies that plagued PC. Jordan once remarked that during the early days, "We never had any problems with lost trains, which had happened on the Penn Central."

After initial changes were implemented in Conrail's first days, alterations to operations were implemented slowly to limit merger trauma. Over time, there were many changes as Conrail consolidated the operations of multiple railroads into one. One of the premises behind Conrail was to reduce the amount of plant and tailor the route structure to better reflect the amount of traffic carried. Yards and locomotive facilities were closed as their functions combined. Conrail's route structure was scaled back to better reflect

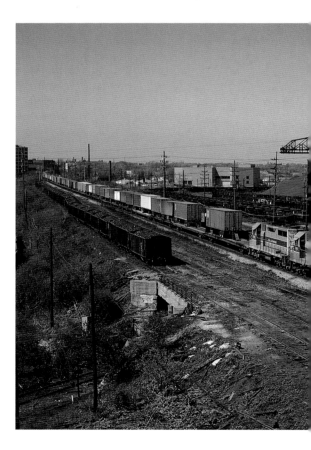

even get a basic 100-mile day out of a crew." Its yards were also in a serious state of disrepair. Some were in such a poor state that switching freight cars resulted in daily derailments.

Not all of Conrail was rebuilt, and Conrail managers generally favored former Penn Central properties as they consolidated the operations of six railroads into one. The former Erie Lackawanna mainlines had dramatic changes. The routes west of Akron, Ohio, didn't fit into Conrail's strategy and most were abandoned. Tower operators' train sheets (logged movement over the railroad) that had been full in March 1976 were nearly empty by May of that year. East of Binghamton, New York, Erie Lackawanna had maintained both former Erie and Lackawanna mainlines to Hoboken and Jersey City. EL operations favored the Lackawanna Line via Scranton, but used both lines for through freight movements. Initially Conrail did the same, but in 1979 it discontinued the Lackawanna Route in favor of the old Erie Delaware

Division, which was known for the famous Starrucca Viaduct.

Furthermore, high-priority traffic was generally diverted off the EL lines and operated over Penn Central routes. West of Hornell, New York, the line was reduced to just three roundtrips a day. Conrail's less-important predecessors quickly lost through traffic. The CNJ, for example, lost all of its east-west traffic, which was shifted to the parallel Lehigh Valley main between Allentown and north Jersey terminals. Likewise, the Lehigh Valley Line west of Allentown lost much of its traffic to other routes. Water Level Route, Lehigh Valley's

A Penn Central EMD leads former Lehigh and Hudson River Alcos shortly after the Conrail merger. *Tim Doherty collection*

29

Former New York Central Alco C430 2056 and a pair Electro-Motive GP9s lead a hopper train across the Ohio River Bridge toward the Pittsburgh Weirton Steel plant in Weirton, West Virginia. Conrail followed Penn Central's practice and assigned Alco Centuries to mineral service runs based in Mingo Junction, Ohio. *Bill Dechau, Doug Eisele collection*

mainline, which had hosted four to five roundtrips daily, was just a shadow. By contrast, the lines east of Allentown remained busy and gradually became busier as Conrail shifted traffic to New York City-area markets off PC routes.

Conrail was quick to de-emphasize PC routes in the Midwest, and several once-busy mainlines were shut down during its first years. The former New York Central Indianapolis–Cincinnati Line was cut, and traffic was routed onto other lines. Operations on the PRR Panhandle Route from Columbus, Ohio, to Chicago was scaled back and foreshadowed Conrail's later attitudes toward PRR Lines West.

Rehabilitation efforts improved mainline conditions, but disrupted service when lines were shut for maintenance. Conrail inherited two mainlines between Indianapolis and St. Louis and planned to consolidate the best portions into one route. During the summer of 1977, crews rebuilt the former PRR line in Illinois and the former NYC line in Indiana. During the reconstruction, freight traffic and Amtrak's National Limited were diverted, which caused horrible delays.

## RAGTAG FLEET

In its early years, Conrail suffered badly from a motive power shortage because of the poor state of its fleet. The October 1977 issue of *TRAINS Magazine* reported that this was Conrail's toughest problem in its first year. The locomotive shortage was a direct result of the hand-to-mouth existence of Conrail's predecessors. Few new locomotives had been acquired, and maintenance had been substandard. Conrail inherited a large number of worn-out locomotives—many dating from the steam-to-diesel transition period.

On day one, approximately 10 percent of Conrail's locomotives were unserviceable. During Conrail's first summer, locomotive availability plummeted. Bad winter weather exacerbated motive power availability, and by December 1976, an estimated 16 percent of its fleet were sidelined.

Except for four orphaned U36bs from Auto Train, Conrail did not obtain new locomotives until 1977, when it ordered 175 units, including 83 EMD SD40-2s. These 3,000-horsepower, six-motor locomotives are considered among the best ever built. As new and rebuilt locomotives arrived, Conrail retired the oldest and least reliable machines.

Initially, Conrail routed north-south traffic on the former PRR electrified lines between Washington D.C. and the New York metro area. Three former PRR GG1, led by 4801, lead a Conrail freight southward near Chesaco Park, Maryland, on October 20, 1978. The GG1s were basically worn out by the time Conrail inherited them and were among the first electrics to be retired. *Doug Eisele*

Conrail rebuilt 1950s-era EMD GP7s and GP9s, which became GP8s and GP10s, respectively. Conrail continued Penn Central's Alco RS-3 rebuild program, which included the replacement of Alco's 244-series engine with EMD's 567 engine.

## WEAK PERFORMANCE DESPITE REBUILGING

The USRA expected Conrail to lose money during its consolidation and rebuilding period. To facilitate Conrail's transformation, the USRA secured billions

Altoona, Pennsylvania, was home to Pennsy's Juniata Locomotive Shops, which became Conrail's primary heavy locomotive shops. This sign was at the entrance to the Juniata Locomotive works at Fourth Avenue in Altoona. Near Altoona, Hollidaysburg was home to Conrail's largest car shops. *Doug Eisele*

By December 1976, Conrail suffered from a motive power shortage because more than 10 percent of its fleet was out of service as a result of serious failures. Conrail leased power from Canadian National and other lines. On December 12, 1976, Canadian National GP40-2Ls were seen west of Dewitt Yard in East Syracuse, New York. Canadian National Locomotives were leased to Conrail for periods of 89 days or less to avoid paying import taxes.
*Doug Eisele*

of dollars in federal capital for reconstruction, new locomotives, and to cover day-to-day operating losses. Unfortunately Conrail's physical condition, traffic density, and financial performance were much worse than the USRA anticipated. It seemed Conrail was off to a good start when its first-year losses were less than forecasted and its rehabilitation programs had exceeded the USRA's goals.

Conrail's admirable progress came to a stall during the winter of 1976–77 when record snowfall and low temperatures wreaked havoc system wide. During January 1977 in Buffalo, one of the worst affected areas, Conrail was forced to fire up its only steam-era rotary snowplow to clear its Niagara Branch and rescue a smaller plow stuck in 15-foot drifts. Earlier in the month, it took four days to remove ice from deep cuts on the old Boston & Albany in Washington, Massachusetts, near the line's summit. Severe weather had exacerbated Conrail's motive power shortage. An estimated 15 percent of its locomotives were out of service that winter because of mechanical failures or required overhaul. According to the USRA, extreme cold sidelined some 200 machines in one

weekend. Conrail estimated that winter-related problems in 1976–77 cost the railroad roughly $100 million.

## CONRAIL IN CRISIS

Despite an influx of billions of federal dollars by the late 1970s, Conrail was in deep trouble. USRA's final system plan had optimistically forecasted that by 1980 Conrail would carry 399 million tons. In actuality, it only carried 237 million tons that year, which was 41 percent less than the USRA plan. By the middle of 1978, it was readily apparent that Conrail was not going to meet the USRA's revenue projections.

In Conrail's traffic projections, the USRA had been overly optimistic and had erred in several key areas. It anticipated that customers lost to service failures would flock back to the railroad once tracks were repaired and services improved. It also hoped that a dramatic rise in coal traffic would boost Conrail's revenue. The USRA had planned for more coal traffic during the oil crisis in 1974–75 and mistakenly anticipated that many oil-fired power plants would be converted to coal.

By 1978, neither of these dreams had transpired. Furthermore, the USRA had not anticipated the deteriorating industrial economy exemplified by the collapse of the domestic steel industry and weakening auto industry, both of which were key Conrail markets. There were other unpredicted factors, too. In 1977, a strike cut iron-ore movements through Great Lakes ports in half.

Even the USRA became critical of Conrail's poor performance when faced with intense political scrutiny, and Conrail's efficiency was brought into question. A June 5, 1978, USRA report to Congress, as reprinted in the August 1978 issue of *TRAINS Magazine*, concluded that, despite a massive influx of federal aid, Conrail didn't have adequate freight-car management. At one point, Conrail had tied up twice as many 50-foot boxcars on its system as the

railroad owned and contributed to a nationwide car shortage.

Delayed shipments and poor transit time discouraged shippers, who abandoned the railroad in favor of faster and more reliable means of transport. According to David P. Morgan in *TRAINS Magazine*, the USRA asserted that Conrail had achieved less than 80 percent of the efficiencies that the USRA had planned.

The USRA concluded that, despite Conrail's improvements, there was "little cause for optimism" that Conrail's operations could become financially self-sufficient by 1980. It further predicted that Conrail would require an additional $1.5 billion to $2.1 billion from 1981 to 1985.

Spending money to repair tracks and locomotives had aimed to cure the symptoms of Conrail's disease, but it did little to address the root causes of its sickness. Conrail's predecessors had stopped maintaining facilities and equipment because they had run out of cash.

Conrail's services were still inadequate. It took too long to deliver cars to customers and cost too much to do so. Although Conrail implemented some route consolidation and plant reduction, it still had too much plant. In addition, Conrail may have squandered some of its maintenance funds to rebuild lines that should have been downgraded or abandoned.

Another factor was that Conrail's labor costs were too high. It had too many employees who produced too little revenue. While the industry as a whole suffered from high labor costs, Conrail was the worst-performing Class 1 American freight railroad. According to the USRA, Conrail spent two-thirds of its revenue on labor in 1978. By comparison, the average Class 1 railroad spent just over half its revenue on labor. In contrast, railroad labor tended to cite examples of

Number 4800, known as Old Rivets, was the prototype Pennsy GG1 that was built in 1934. It was also the only GG1 to be painted Conrail Blue. It is seen inside the former PRR shops in Wilmington, Delaware. By 1981, Conrail 4800 had been retired and sent to be displayed at the Railroad Museum of Pennsylvania in Strasburg. It was subsequently repainted in an early PRR livery. *John Scala, Patrick Yough collection*

inexperienced, incompetent, or inept railroad management. Regardless of the problem's source, the reality was that American railroads suffered from antiquated, inefficient work practices. In the December 1978 issue of *TRAINS Magazine*, David P. Morgan pointed out that, "[Penn Central] couldn't afford to confront its Brotherhoods about work rules the railroad couldn't afford."

Although poor labor utilization characterized the railroad's inefficient practices, Conrail faced additional inefficiencies. One problem was the result of the shift in the northeastern economy. Traditionally, heavy manufacturing had brought in raw materials and sent out manufactured goods. As manufacturing left the region, the Northeast became the terminus for more traffic than it produced. The effect was that a growing amount of freight cars were loaded eastbound and were empty westbound. The empty westbound moves contributed to the perceived car shortage and lowered revenue.

Conrail management was not oblivious to the company's woes, and Edward Jordan was keenly aware of Conrail's failings. He believed fundamental issues needed to be

A Conrail safety sign at the Cresson, Pennsylvania, helper base features a graphic representation of an Electro-Motive GP30. *Brian Solomon*

addressed before Conrail could achieve self-sufficiency. He said, "Conrail is losing a dime on every dollar of freight revenue it takes in. Obviously, Conrail has too much unprofitable traffic on too much plant." He further explained that the existing regulations for rate-making and abandonment procedures were the root cause of Conrail's losses. Market forces, rather than government policies and regulations, should determine

the level, quality, and geographic demands for Conrail's service. Jordan's solution to make Conrail profitable was to eliminate government rate regulation and simplify the abandonment process.

Conrail's poor performance was a specific mandate for railroad rate deregulation. In four years, Conrail spent $3 billion in federal aid, yet had not attained profitability. Unless fundamental changes were made to the rate structure, many feared that Conrail would indefinitely drain federal funds. Worse, in light of Conrail's dreadful performance, there were renewed fears that the whole industry was on the verge of total collapse, despite record levels of freight tonnage nationwide. The poor return rate was a symptom that seemed to indicate that even the profitable lines would become basket cases.

Although total freedom to set prices was not granted to the industry, compromise legislation was drafted that ultimately paved the way for the revitalization of the railroad industry. The Staggers Rail Act was passed by Congress and signed by President Jimmy Carter on October 14, 1980. Among other things, the Staggers Act instructed the ICC to remove rate regulation from many types of rail traffic.

## LIGHT AT THE END OF THE TUNNEL?

By the end of 1980, Conrail had started to emerge from the gloom. It still had many critics, and talk of breaking up the company continued, but the situation was not as desperate as it had seemed two years earlier. Conrail had accomplished some goals set forth by the 3-R Act and the USRA. Its physical plant had been rehabilitated, and its customers were getting more reliable freight service than had been offered by Conrail's predecessors. In January 1981, Fred W. Frailey quantified Conrail's rebuilding in *TRAINS Magazine*. Conrail had installed 3,873 miles of new rail, replaced 18.4 million

A Conrail U25b leads a freight along the old Shoreline route near New Haven, Connecticut, in December 1979. The New Haven Railroad used unusual short-blade, left-hand semaphores in its electrified territory. A few of these distinctive signals survived until the early 1980s. In the wake of the Staggers Act, Conrail discontinued many unprofitable through services on its former New Haven routes. *Don Marson*

Rick Frey
KELLY Fisher

These E-33 electrics were built for Virginian and worked for four owners before Conrail. The E33 was the first electric to use the road-switcher configuration. A pair of E33s have departed the former PRR Enola Yard and are humming through West Fairview, Pennsylvania, on March 9, 1980. Conrail electric operations ceased in 1981. One of the E33s was preserved in the Virginian livery in Roanoke, Virginia. *Doug Eisele*

ties, and surfaced 35,385 miles of track since 1976. More than 3,000 locomotives were overhauled or rebuilt, and 675 new locomotives were purchased. More important than these statistics, Conrail's service was much better, and with rehabilitated plant, locomotives, and cars, it finally had the tools needed to move forward.

But Conrail's biggest stumbling block was its continuing poor financial state.

Conrail remained unprofitable and required federal capital to fund major projects and cover operational losses. The Jordan regime ended in 1980 with the arrival of L. Stanley Crane.

# CHAPTER THREE

# LET CONRAIL
# BE CONRAIL

## *Conrail's Knight in Shining Armor*

Professionally, L. Stanley Crane was the antithesis of Edward Jordan. Jordan had

been brought in to lead Conrail because he was an outsider who admittedly knew little about

railroading and was free from traditional bias. Crane was a lifelong railroader, well respected in

the industry, and had recently retired as the head of the Southern Railway.

Crane had retired because he had reached the Southern's arbitrary mandatory retirement age.

He wasn't ready to leave the railroad business and looked for a new challenge after he left Southern.

Crane later described his tenure at Conrail between 1981 and 1988 in a speech to the Newcomen

Society. Crane praised Conrail and the leadership his predecessor had put in place. Remarkably,

Crane brought none of his own people to Conrail and worked with the existing management.

In January 1980, Conrail added the slogan "Keep it moving with Conrail" to General Electric B23-7 1980. When Conrail's traffic declined in the early 1980s, it placed hundreds of locomotives in storage. On September 16, 1984, 1980 leads CLBU (Cleveland to Buffalo) near the train's terminal. By 1984, the economy improved and Conrail experienced its largest profit. *Doug Eisele*

## DAWN OF A NEW ERA

Crane arrived at Conrail in January 1981 just as Ronald Reagan took office as President of the United States, which spelled big changes for Conrail. On February 18, 1981, the Reagan administration proposed large cuts in federal aid to railroads. This was mainly aimed toward funding for Conrail, Amtrak, the Northeast Corridor Improvement Project, and low-density freight lines. The Reagan administration suggested that Conrail could operate without federal aid if it abandoned lines, cut employment, and sought state and local support.

Crane used one of the lesser-known provisions of the Staggers Act that required a detailed analysis of Conrail to be carried out by the USDOT, USRA, and the railroad itself for submission to Congress. Conrail's analysis was called "Options for Conrail" and provided an opportunity for Conrail's management to present its own plan for the future that would address the structural challenges needed to attain profitability. Submitted on April 1, 1981, Crane's vision for profitability called for "unconventional changes and improvements [that] must be implemented." These changes included a mandate for additional line abandonment, cuts in the labor force, substantial changes in work rules, and state support for marginal lines. Since many of these changes were beyond Conrail's control, they would have to be included in new legislation that needed to be passed by Congress and signed by President Reagan.

## PLAYING POLITICS

To keep Conrail from being immediately sold to the highest bidder, Crane and Conrail would have to engineer a multifaceted deal with the Reagan administration and Congress between April and August 1981. As part of this deal, Conrail would have to gain concessions from labor unions and receive the structural changes it requested in the "Options for Conrail" that would allow profitability.

Drew Lewis, secretary of transportation, made it clear to Crane that the Reagan administration planned to liquidate Conrail and scrap what it could not sell. Crane

Conrail series N-21 Caboose 21284 is at the back of a local freight working the West Shore Branch at the Genessee Junction Yard south of Rochester, New York. The N-21 was the only series of caboose bought new by Conrail. All of the others were inherited from its predecessors. Conrail began dispensing cabooses in 1984, and by the late 1980s, most through trains operated without them. Some locals retained cabooses for switching moves. *Brian Solomon*

argued that an independent Conrail could make it on its own without perpetual federal aid. He brought his arguments directly to the White House and convinced federal budget director David Stockman that Conrail would only require another $300 million over the following two years to cover continuing deficits. After that, the company would operate profitability without the need for further subsidy. This amount was substantially less than the government thought it would need to survive. Even the USRA had suggested that Conrail would need an additional $2 billion by 1985.

With the funding commitment from the White House, Crane and Lewis made a deal with the Reagan administration in 1983 to postpone plans to sell Conrail if it could meet two economic tests of its profitability.

If Conrail failed the tests, it would be sold in pieces to the highest bidders. If it

passed them, the railroad could stay together. Before this deal could be finalized, Conrail sought concessions from labor. Conrail was paying wage rates based on national agreements that covered profitable railroads, but Conrail's labor costs were significantly higher than those of the profitable railroads.

Crane and other Conrail executives made a detailed analysis starting with the amount of money that had to be cut from costs and then subtracted what could be realistically cut from each area. They determined that labor needed to be cut by $200 million a year for three years.

The labor unions agreed to the cuts because selling the railroad piecemeal was not in their best interest. Labor leaders worked with Conrail management to produce an agreement that deferred 12 percent of cost increases in new national rail labor contracts

Three C30-7As and a C32-8, both GE 12-cylinder six-motor models unique to Conrail, lead SEPW-X (Selkirk to Providence & Worcester-extra) at the State Line Tunnel at 9:38 a.m. on May 29, 1988. By the end of the year, Conrail completed its single tracking of the Boston Line at this location, and the track in the foreground was removed from regular service. Today, only one of State Line's twin-bores carries tracks. *Brian Solomon*

Conrail drastically reduced the amount of interchange traffic moving through Buffalo. Many pre-Conrail yards were abandoned. A local passes the remains of a Lehigh Valley yard at Tifft Street. *Brian Solomon*

A Conrail GP10 works the west end of Enola Yard on July 28, 1988. Conrail's GP10s were rebuilt from Electro-Motive GP9s. GP10 was a Conrail designation and not an official Electro-Motive model number. *Brian Solomon*

for three years. This agreement gave Crane the savings he asked for.

After obtaining concessions from labor, Crane needed congressional approval for his agreement with Drew Lewis. Conrail's friends in Congress attached the legislation to a required federal budget bill that passed both houses of Congress and was signed by President Reagan on August 13, 1981. The legislation, known as the Northeast Rail Service Act (NERSA), facilitated Conrail's departure from the passenger business, eased abandonment regulations to make it easier and cheaper to abandon lines, provided state and local tax exemption, and funded payments to idled railway employees to end the lifetime job protection provided under the 3-R Act.

## FORGING NEW TRAFFIC PATTERNS

Crane's first months as Conrail chairman involved political battles in Washington to secure Conrail's future as a single entity. He traveled the system for days to make traffic assessments and plan where to trim physical plant.

To further complicate matters, Conrail faced a serious recession when Crane assumed control. Just because a line or yard was quiet in 1981 didn't necessarily mean it was inessential, or that a heavily traveled

route needed to be retained. Careful, calculated analysis was needed to make cuts for the greatest gains. If Crane cut unwisely, he might hinder the railroad's recovery when the economy improved.

Crane was swift and calculating in his assessments. Following an office car inspection trip over the former Pennsy Panhandle mainline between Pittsburgh and Columbus, Crane ordered that through traffic be diverted and the line downgraded. This drastic move was barely noticed by the railroad press at the time. What caught public attention was lifting the No. 2 mainline around the Horseshoe Curve in March 1981.

These were just two examples of Crane's pruning of Conrail. Throughout the system, duplicate and redundant tracks and lines were downgraded, abandoned, and lifted

while traffic shifted. Trains were rerouted onto core routes.

In another related move in the Northeast, traffic was shifted off the former PRR's electrified lines onto former Lehigh Valley and Reading routes to avoid high Amtrak charges. As a result of this shift, Conrail sidelined its electric fleet and relegated its dozens of E44s and E33s to storage at Enola. Under Crane, the day of electric freight came to an end, and hardly anyone noticed or complained.

## CONRAIL FINALLY OBTAINS SAVINGS FROM MERGED LINES

The great unfulfilled promise of the Penn Central merger was the savings obtained by eliminating duplicate lines and creating new efficient routes by combining the best parts of

Between 1982 and 1984, Conrail's Empire State Xpress competed directly with trucking via the New York State Thruway between Buffalo and New York. This was Conrail's first application of RoadRailers technology. RoadRailer had contracted Conrail to run the service. Conrail routinely assigned its four U36Bs to the RoadRailers, which were largely nocturnal. The eastward RRT-12 rolls through Rochester, New York, on June 8, 1983. Conrail's U36Bs were built for Auto Train, but were sold to Conrail as its first new locomotives. *Doug Eisele*

Conrail C30-7 leads a southward UNL-146 unit train over the Corning Secondary near Tioga, Pennsylvania, on September 29, 1986. On this day, in addition to 83 empty coal hoppers from the power plant at the end of the Ithaca Secondary, the train consists of 4 autoracks and 34 mixed freight cars. This portion of the Corning Secondary was relocated to accommodate a dam. In 1988, Conrail closed the Corning–Newberry Junction portion of the line to through traffic in favor of the former PRR Buffalo Line. *Doug Eisele*

By the mid-1980s, Conrail was the largest intermodal carrier in the United States. The former New York Central Water Level Route was Conrail's premiere intermodal corridor. In April 1987, Conrail intermodal trains pause at Dewitt Yard, east of Syracuse, New York. In the 1990s, Conrail developed Dewitt as its regional intermodal hub. *Brian Solomon*

the both railroads, but Penn Central had been stymied. It had faced a hostile abandonment process and onerous labor agreements that precluded significant savings from trimmed plant. Empowered by regulatory changes provided by the Northeast Rail Services Act that simplified the abandonment process, Conrail conducted a rationalization similar to what was envisioned by Penn Central's architects.

In 1982, Conrail's annual report explained that it was completing the first phase of an expedited abandonment process involving 2,600 route miles of track that only generated 1 percent of the company's revenue. More than 700 miles were sold to shortline railroads that operated the tracks and fed traffic to Conrail. Since shortlines had lower costs and proved more capable of marketing rail service than Conrail, the arrangements were usually beneficial to all parties, shippers included.

In addition to light branchlines, Conrail's rationalization efforts hacked away at duplicate through routes. By the time Conrail was done, little of the old PRR west of the Ohio River remained integral to the Conrail system.

Conrail's BUOI-4X is seen in East Hornell, New York, at the site of the former Erie Railroad yard on January 14, 1989. Conrail's BUOI operated daily between Frontier Yard in Buffalo, New York, and Oak Island, New Jersey, along the Southern Tier route. While it carried through freight, BUOI was effectively a long distance local that made pickups and setouts along the way. The X in this train's designation indicates it is an extra-BUOI, which means another train with the same symbol will run on this day. Freshly shopped New York City subway cars from the Hornell Shops are at the front of the train. *Brian Solomon*

In the first few years, the simplified abandonment procedures of NERSA allowed Conrail to trim 4,400 route miles that sacrificed 1 percent of the railroad traffic and 2 percent of revenue.

## THE GREAT LOCOMOTIVE GARAGE SALE

In 1981, Conrail had 4,156 locomotives, 15 percent of which were in the United States. Over the next 3 years, Conrail retired, sold, or transferred 1,265 of its locomotives, a 30-percent fleet reduction.

As a result of having fewer locomotives, the former New York Central locomotive shop in Collinwood was closed, and Conrail concentrated heavy maintenance work at Altoona's Juniata Shops. Many of the 350 displaced workers were reassigned to the expanded Collinwood terminal.

## CONRAIL ECLIPSED

While Conrail abandoned unnecessary track and sold or scrapped unneeded motive power, Burlington Northern and Union Pacific both eclipsed Conrail in the number of locomotives, route miles, and revenue. They expanded through mergers and acquisition (BN bought Frisco; UP merged with Missouri Pacific and Western Pacific). Meanwhile in the East, two new giants emerged. Chessie System joined with the Family Lines railroads (Seaboard Coast Line, Louisville & Nashville, and affiliated railroads) to form CSX. Norfolk & Western merged with Southern Railway to form Norfolk Southern. Conrail had been the largest railroad in America in 1976, but by the mid-1980s, it had shrunk and found itself surrounded by newly created giants.

## LAST TRAIN AT PLATFORM 21

In its first years, Conrail acted as a contract carrier for Amtrak and Commuter Authorities, and was the nation's largest passenger carrier. It operated passenger lines in the New York and Philadelphia metropolitan areas and in New Jersey, Connecticut, and Maryland.

The Northeast Rail Services Act mandated that Conrail discontinue passenger business

by December 31, 1982. New transit agencies were created by New York, New Jersey, and Connecticut to assume former Conrail operations. In Philadelphia, SEPTA, the existing agency, stepped in.

Amtrak was also affected by the NERSA train and engine crews that had worked on the Northeast Corridor Amtrak Routes and became Amtrak employees. Conrail's 1982 annual report indicated that 11,000 people were cut from its workforce as a result of these transfers.

### RAILS TO TRAILS

As Conrail was downsizing, it also needed to better serve existing customers and new markets. Many changes were made possible as a result of the Staggers Act.

Deregulation had a profound effect on Conrail and the rest of the railroad industry. Railroads were given many new opportunities and challenges. Union Pacific's now-retired chairman, John C. Kenefick

(also a vice president for New York Central in his early years), was quoted in the September 1986 *TRAINS Magazine.*

*"In the days before deregulation, about the only thing a railroad could sell was service and a smile. You couldn't do anything about price with prices, so you paid close attention to your service and that's the way you got business. Now service and a smile count, but deregulation means you've got to deliver price. I've found that the sweetest smile in the world won't count if your competitor is 5 cents under you."*

In the new deregulated environment, railroads were free to act like other businesses. They could set prices, refuse unprofitable business, tailor service, and make longterm contracts with customers. With the help of deregulation, the industry made it through the recession in the early

1980s without incurring a single new bankruptcy. Although the recession slowed the effect of Staggers, by the mid-1990s, the railroad industry had been transformed. Some hailed it as the second golden age of American railroading.

## INTERMODAL GIANT

Conrail had a near monopoly on rail transport to the nation's largest concentrated consumer markets: the cities of the Northeast. To best serve these markets, Conrail developed its intermodal service—

trailer on flatcar (TOFC) and containers on flatcar (COFC). Intermodal allowed the railroad to profitably transport high-value consumer goods. Deregulation enabled Conrail to aggressively compete with truckers and recapture business lost over the previous decades. During the 1980s, Conrail emerged as the largest intermodal carrier in the United States.

## LET CONRAIL BE CONRAIL

In 1981, Conrail's fortunes had begun to improve. Crane's efforts at cost control improved the company's cash flow. At the end of the year, Conrail had made its first full-year profit, $39 million. Profits continued in 1982, and by 1983, Conrail met the first of the profitability tests required by the 1981 NERSA legislation. Soon after the company demonstrated profitability, labor leaders representing Conrail employees made an offer to buy Conrail for $500 million. Convinced of Conrail's profitability, potential buyers cropped up everywhere.

One of the operational bottlenecks on the Southern Tier route was 25 miles of 10 miles per hour slow orders on the eastward main track between River Junction, near Dalton, New York, and Hornell. In April 1989, Conrail BUOI, led by SD50 6793, switches a customer in Hornell, New York, after it traversed the slow eastward main. Running against the current of traffic and around BUOI on the westward main, DHT-4C, a Delaware & Hudson Sealand double-stack is led by Susquehanna DASH 8-40B 4002. This train will cross over to the eastward main at CP East Hornell and continue east through the Canisteo Valley with the current of traffic on the eastward track. *Brian Solomon*

In the late 1980s, the Southern Tier was the preferred route for double-stack trains to the East Coast. At 8:35 a.m. on January 22, 1989, Conrail TV200X, led by GP40-2 3403, bumps along at 10 miles per hour on the No.2 track (eastward main) near Swain, New York. American Presidents Line double-stack service began in 1984. Conrail assigned new symbols to its APL trains and moved them from the TV300 series to the TV200 series in 1988. *Brian Solomon*

At this time, Crane's vision for Conrail's future was that either a large financially solid company should buy it, or it should remain independent through a sale to public shareholders. Crane approached Santa Fe and believed an end-to-end merger with that railroad would preserve the most jobs.

Santa Fe was initially interested and started negotiations with Conrail, but it soon lost interest when it opted to pursue Southern Pacific (the merger between Santa Fe and SP was later rejected by the ICC on antitrust grounds).

Potential buyers eagerly waited to see if Conrail passed its second profitability test in December 1983. When it did, Secretary of Transportation Elizabeth Dole, who had taken over for Drew Lewis, sought to take Conrail to the private sector. Dole and the Department of Transportation thought the best way to recoup the government's investment in Conrail, and to preserve the railroad, was to encourage its sale to a profitable carrier with sufficiently deep pockets to withstand the next inevitable downturn. Newly

formed railroads Norfolk Southern and CSX both expressed interest in acquiring Conrail.

By the June 1984 deadline, the Department of Transportation had received 18 different bids for Conrail. Investment houses, railroad labor, and Norfolk Southern had all bid. DOTs criteria for bid evaluation included leaving Conrail in the strongest possible position after the sale; maintaining service levels to communities and shippers; and recouping as much of the government's substantial investment in Conrail as possible, while meeting the other criteria. A day after bids were due, a Department of Transportation official gave Crane and Conrail an opening by saying that the government might accept a sale to the public through an initial public offering.

Dole and the DOT carefully assessed all bids and recommended that the Norfolk Southern offer be selected. Not everyone agreed. CSX Chairman Hay T. Watkins said to Congress:

*"We made a careful study of a possible purchase by CSX and concluded there*

A Conrail inspection train pauses on the recently rebuilt wye at South Station in Boston in December 1987. Today this whole scene has changed. The electrification of the Northeast Corridor, combined with the construction of a parking garage and bus terminal over South Station and changes because of Boston's Big Dig, have greatly altered the infrastructure.
*Brian Solomon*

would be a great benefit to CSX. After all, Conrail is a very significant customer and competitor of CSX, and buying Conrail would eliminate that competition and forever capture the traffic for CSX, which now flows from Conrail. We also concluded that very much of the same analysis would apply to Norfolk Southern. It only pays to be a monopolist if you can get away with it. Our study convinced us that a CSX or Norfolk Southern proposal to buy Conrail would not survive any rational scrutiny under the antitrust concepts that have governed every railroad merger in this country."

Faced with losing as much as $400 million from a Conrail–NS merger, CSX threatened to abandon B&O rather than attempt to compete with the merged company. For

Conrail, the selection of Norfolk Southern meant that many workers who had just sacrificed to make the railroad profitable would likely lose their jobs.

In the meantime, Crane took advantage of the previous opening and presented a plan with its now famous slogan, "Let Conrail Be Conrail." The proposal stated that the company would remain independent with its existing management and that its shares would be sold, over time, to the public. Crane described the ensuing conflict over Conrail's future as trench warfare. Between October 1984, when Conrail first announced its intention to seek an independent sale, and August 1986, when that matter was effectively resolved in Congress, Conrail and its various supporters in labor, business, and Congress lined up on one side, while Conrail's foes at the

Conrail SD50 6710 and three other EMDs have made a set out of cars on the former West Shore south of Rochester. This section of the former West Shore provided a bypass for the Chicago Line south of Rochester as well as a connection to the short line Lavoina Avon & Lakeville. *Brian Solomon*

Department of Transportation and Norfolk Southern lined up on the other side.

Finally, the administration's plan to sell Conrail to Norfolk Southern hit an insurmountable obstacle, Congressman John Dingell, chairman of the powerful House Energy and Commerce Committee. Any legislation to approve a sale would have to pass through this committee. Congressman Dingell, whose district in Michigan was served by Conrail, spoke out against the sale and saw significant anticompetitive/antitrust aspects, as well as the favorable terms for Norfolk Southern as Conrail continued to prosper. Even after NS raised its bid to $1.9 billion in May 9, 1986, the congressman presented a plan to sell the railroad to the public as an independent entity. Not wanting to antagonize Congress any further, Norfolk Southern withdrew its bid on August 19, 1986.

On March 26, 1987, a few days shy of Conrail's 11th birthday, the federal government's share in Conrail was sold as an initial public offering on the New York Stock Exchange for $1.645 billion before fees. The sale of 58,750,000 shares at $28 per share was the largest initial public offering up until that that time. After NS pulled out its bid in August 1986, the Department of Transportation agreed to the public sale, and Congress passed the authorizing legislation, which was signed by President Reagan on October 21. With the sale, Conrail ended its second phase of existence to begin public ownership and experience the whims of the market.

The additional $300 million that the Reagan administration offered Crane in 1981 was never spent and remained in the federal treasury.

# CHAPTER FOUR

# INTO THE BLACK

During the late 1980s and early 1990s, the transportation industry underwent significant changes that reflected the global nature of the industries it supported. As a result, Conrail was in a state of flux. L. Stanley Crane retired in 1988, after he successfully led and won the campaign for Conrail's independence through a public stock offering. Amidst an unexpected leadership crisis and economic recession, the company faced an internal struggle over how to grow its business.

As a privately owned company responsible to individual stockholders rather than the federal government, Conrail faced the complexities of maximizing shareholder value of its stock. Conrail needed to carefully weigh long-term planning against the short-term demands needed for quarterly profits. This is a tricky balance, and at times, counterintuitive in railroading.

Conrail was the only railroad to buy EMD's SD80MAC. The SD80MAC was a three-phase AC traction model unique to Conrail that was powered by a 20–cylinder, 710 diesel-engine. Conrail operated 30 of them, numbered 4100 to 4129. On May 24, 1997, a pair of SD80MACs lead TV9 through the Twin Ledges rock cuttings on the east slope of Washington Hill, west of Middlefield, Massachusetts. *Brian Solomon*

## MANAGEMENT CRISIS

The former PRR mainline across Pennsylvania was one of Conrail's busiest routes. In November 1998, six months before Conrail was split by Norfolk Southern and CSX, a pair of SD40-2s helpers shove on the back of a heavy freight as a eastward RoadRailer climbs on an adjacent track in Portage, Pennsylvania. Conrail and NS jointly operated RoadRailer intermodal trains for several years prior to the Conrail breakup. Today, the former PRR mainline line seen here is operated by NS. *Brian Solomon*

After L. Stanley Crane retired from Conrail at age 73 in 1988, Richard D. Sanborn, a former CSX executive and a talented, well-respected railroader with much promise, succeeded him. Sanborn died unexpectedly a few months after he was appointed. Conrail then recruited another CSX man and former Conrail executive to lead the company. James A. Hagen took over from interim chairman Stanley Hillman on May 18, 1989.

Former Conrail executive Larry DeYoung gave an insightful insider's look at Conrail's management in the January 1999 issue of *TRAINS Magazine,* explaining how Hagen imposed a new management structure on Conrail's traditional railroad organization. Hagen brought a new strategic plan to develop new business, improved service, and controlled costs. His strategy set significant new revenue goals for Conrail and looked to improve economic efficiency.

Unfortunately, the recession of the late 1980s and 1990s limited Conrail's opportunity for growth.

To survive in a modern economy, Conrail needed to grow its business to increase revenue and return on investment, and significantly reduce its costs while it maintained profitability. To expand its business, Conrail made strategic purchases, most notably the coal-hauling Monongahela Railroad in 1990. However, Conrail management was more experienced in cost cutting than revenue growth. This was the product of the railroad's decade-long struggle for profitability and independence. Conrail continued to shrink employment as it trimmed unprofitable and marginally profitable routes, and simplified its management structure.

The railroad made a continued investment in its physical plant and motive power. At the end of December 1993, Conrail operated 11,831 route miles that

consisted of 20,109 miles of track. Of this, 6,276 track miles, which annually carried 10 million gross tons of freight, were laid with heavyweight rail that weighed 127 pounds per yard, and 98 percent was continuous-welded rail, which reduces track maintenance costs. Conrail maintained 5,647 track miles for fast freight traffic with a speed of 50 miles per hour or faster, and an estimated 33 percent of these lines had a maximum freight speed of 70 miles per hour. Conrail estimated that 7,610 miles of the track moved 10 million gross tons annually and was protected by automatic signal systems.

Between 1991 and 1996, Conrail replaced most of its older power with new locomotives from General Electric and General Motors' Electro-Motive Division. The average age of the Conrail locomotive fleet decreased from 15.3 years to 11.1 years, and fleet size decreased from 2,187 to 2,006 between 1993 and 1996.

## MEGAMERGER MANIA

In 1994, the North American railroad scene entered a tumultuous period as a

*Above:* On July 27, 1988, a Conrail maintenance gang welds a rail near MG Tower on the grade between Altoona and Gallitzin, Pennsylvania. One of most dramatic differences between Conrail and its predecessors was its well maintained mainlines. *Brian Solomon*

*Left:* Conrail operations on the Boston Line typically ran eastward trains over the line in the morning. On April 30, 1997, SD50 6742 leads an eastward intermodal train through the fog along the Quaboag River east of Palmer, Massachusetts, near CP79 (east end of a controlled siding installed in 1986). *Brian Solomon*

series of massive mergers were proposed. Since the big mergers of mid-1980s, there had only been minor changes in the North American rail map. The eight American Class 1 railroads and the two big Canadian companies controlled most mainline mileage and traffic.

In June 1994, Burlington Northern and Santa Fe announced plans to merge. This spurred a counteroffer for the Santa Fe, by Union Pacific (UP), Burlington Northern's archrival, and set a number of other merger proposals in motion. Burlington Northern triumphed over UP and ultimately merged with Santa Fe. Union Pacific responded by merging with its longtime interchange partner, the

Chicago & North Western, and going after the Southern Pacific a few years later.

In the wake of the BNSF announcement, Illinois Central and Kansas City Southern announced that they were considering a merger. In August 1994, word came out that Norfolk Southern and Conrail had also been in merger talks. Conrail, which would later decide against a merger with NS, appointed President David M. LeVan as the successor to Chairman James Hagan in September 1994, and announced that the railroad was not for sale.

With its path clear, Conrail focused its efforts toward further trimming costs in order to boost its return on investment. In September 1994, Conrail exited short and

The first day that CSX and Norfolk Southern could exercise control over Conrail, which they had jointly purchased, was August 22, 1998. Until then, they were barred from exerting control over Conrail operations. On that evening, Conrail's SEAL (Selkirk to Allentown) rolls across Iona Island on the River Line. The official split of Conrail occurred at the end of May 1999.
*Tim Doherty*

medium distance intermodal markets to free track capacity for more profitable, longer distance moves.

In 1995, Conrail identified 4,000 miles of track for possible sale that would essentially leave Conrail with its core mainlines. These mainlines, known as the Big X, consisted of the primary east-west routes between Chicago and St Louis' lines to the East Coast ports (Boston, New York, Philadelphia, and Baltimore), which crossed at Cleveland. Virtually all other routes were considered for possible sale.

At the same time, Conrail management reviewed different options for market expansion. They set aggressive strategic financial goals and thought they could be reached by attracting new traffic to its existing routes while improving operational efficiency. Conrail considered various possible acquisitions including Illinois Central, which proved more expensive than Conrail was willing to pay.

## CONRAIL VIES FOR THE COTTON BELT
On August 3, 1995, Union Pacific offered $5.4 billion for Southern Pacific (SP).

Initially, Union Pacific indicated it might sell some lines to preserve competition.

Conrail executives believed that Southern Pacific's Cotton Belt subsidiary was an ideal addition to the Conrail system. With tracks between Texas and the Gulf Coast, the Cotton Belt interchanged considerable chemical and plastic traffic with Conrail. A sale to Conrail would allow this traffic to move over a unified route, and eliminate delays and cost inefficiencies incurred through interchange. Other efficiencies could also be gained, such as using Conrail's maintenance crews and equipment on the Cotton Belt's warm-weather lines during the winter.

Union Pacific rejected Conrail's offer of $1.9 billion for the Cotton Belt in June 1996 and decided to work with BNSF on an extensive trackage rights agreement. Undeterred, Conrail made an outright offer for Cotton Belt and launched an aggressive campaign to convince shippers to oppose the merger, and ultimately, took its case to the Surface Transportation Board (STB), the regulatory agency that was formed to succeed the Interstate Commerce

The eastern entrance of Oak Island Yard can only be reached by crossing Upper Bay Bridge across Newark Bay. This unusual view of a Conrail manifest crossing the bridge against the scenic Manhattan skyline was made from breakdown lane on the New Jersey Turnpike. *Tim Doherty*

Commission (ICC). The STB did not inherit most of the bureaucracy or regulatory power once commanded by the ICC. It had one significant power—to oversee and approve railroad mergers.

Union Pacific Chairman Drew Lewis was a Washington insider and used his connections to aggressively lobby for the UP and SP merger. Conrail raised important anticompetitive issues with UP/SP and pointed out that the combined company would have a 90 percent monopoly on tracks and traffic between the Midwest and the Texas Gulf Coast. Conrail hoped the government regulators would address this issue and force a sale of the Cotton Belt as a condition of the merger. Rather than submit a detailed opposing application or an offer for the Cotton Belt, which regulators would have been forced to evaluate, Conrail opted for this purely anticompetitive objection with the STB.

A June 4, 1996, *Washington Post* article listed three federal agencies, including the Department of Transportation, that believed portions of the combined UP/SP should be sold to maintain competition. The Justice Department said the merger would give "UP a monopoly in hundreds of markets, including Houston and the Gulf Coast," which were served by the Cotton Belt.

Despite these arguments, on July 3, 1996, the Surface Transportation Board approved the Union Pacific and Southern Pacific merger with agreed BNSF trackage rights in a unanimous decision that rejected every major concession requested by other railroads, including Conrail.

## CONRAIL IN THE WAKE OF UP/SP

Losing the Cotton Belt option put Conrail at a critical juncture. Since its inception in 1976, it had consistently shrunk its physical plant. By 1996, Conrail had trimmed its network to a trunk core. Its greatest asset had been its controversial rail monopoly on Northeast markets, but this asset was less relevant as competition using rail and non-rail means penetrated markets in the region, and freight transportation took on a more global approach.

Transportation specialist Don Phillips said in a July 4, 1996, *Washington Post* article that the approval of UP/SP would spur a new round of railroad mergers as the two new large western carriers sought to create transcontinental systems. The perceived imbalance between east and west complicated the execution of a final round of mergers. Following UP/SP, there were two huge systems in the west, and three in the east. If UP paired with CSX, and BNSF with NS, Conrail feared it might be left out of the transcontinental merger movement. This would have greatly damaged the company and its shareholders. To overcome this difficulty, Conrail suggested a sale to CSX that would preserve its hold on the Northeast and benefit its shareholders.

A *Washington Post* profile of CSX Chairman John Snow recounted how Conrail Chairman David LeVan was "weary of fighting off advances from Norfolk Southern" and offered to sell Conrail to CSX in September 1996. Prior to this, Snow had downplayed CSX's interest in Conrail, but suddenly Conrail provided an opportunity to greatly expand CSX and give great access to the largest consumer market in the Northeast. Furthermore, LeVan argued that

the railroad operating cultures of CSX and Conrail matched more closely than either company did with NS. This implied a Conrail merger with CSX would be easier to integrate than with NS. This was important considering the Penn Central debacle was related to operational incompatibility.

Together, Conrail and CSX would be able to compete for north-south traffic originating and terminating in East Coast cities. This was a reversal of policy, since traditional Conrail argued its greatest profit was on long-distance, east-west traffic.

## THE FIGHT FOR CONRAIL

CSX and Conrail announced on October 14, 1996, that CSX would purchase Conrail for a stock and cash offer that totaled more than $8.1 billion. Before the effect of this announcement could settle in, Norfolk Southern responded with a counteroffer of $9.1 billion.

Newspapers, including *The Washington Post*, reported that CSX and Conrail executives were shocked that NS countered so quickly. Don Phillips quoted one NS executive as saying, "John [Snow] thought we'd be

a bunch of timid southern gentlemen." CSX seemed to expect that NS would accept the CSX–Conrail deal sitting down. In retrospect, it would have been more surprising if NS had not reacted. The CSX–Conrail merger would have greatly limited its potential for partners, and NS feared being left out. Norfolk Southern retained more than $1 billion in cash to take advantage of a buying opportunity.

Norfolk Southern's counteroffer led to a costly bidding war for Conrail that lasted until January 1997. In order to avoid STB arbitration, NS and CSX decided to divide Conrail among themselves before they sought merger approval from the STB.

The terms of CSX's agreement for the Conrail purchase barred it from splitting the railroad with NS. Anticompetitive issues were at the crux of the purchase quandary, since whichever railroad ultimately bought Conrail would have a rail stranglehold on northeastern markets. Without Conrail, NS and CSX were roughly equal competitors in the region, but the line that controlled Conrail would become the dominant player in the east.

Conrail TV-6 approaches the summit of the Boston Line's Washington Hill on October 10, 1997. By 1996, Conrail's Boston line was one of the few major Conrail intermodal routes that could not accommodate maximum height double-stacks. The 19 foot clearances on the line limited stack trains to older international containers that could only travel as far east as Worchester. *Tim Doherty*

59

Instead of bringing the decision to the STB, Conrail shareholders solved the immediate issue by rejecting the CSX offer on January 17, 1997. This effectively allowed CSX and NS to negotiate a deal that divided Conrail between them. On March 7, 1997, NS and CSX announced their intention to split Conrail.

## CONRAIL DIVIDED

Norfolk Southern took 57 percent of Conrail routes, and CSX took 43 percent. In his book *Railroad Mergers*, Frank Wilner states that, with the CSX–NS deal, Conrail shareholders received $10.2 billion in cash—a record selling price for a railroad. The stock, which sold for $14 a share in 1987, was purchased at $115 a share in 1997.

In June 1997, CSX and NS filed with the STB their plan to split Conrail. The eight-volume, 14,810-page report detailed which assets each railroad would gain and what measures would ensure competition after the merger.

CSX gained the remaining former New York Central routes between New York and New England as far west as Cleveland, plus the St. Louis Line, the western end of the Fort Wayne Line, the Toledo–Columbus Route, and the route between Philadelphia and Newark. Norfolk Southern gained most remaining former Pennsy lines in Pennsylvania, plus related Lehigh Valley and some Reading routes in eastern Pennsylvania and New Jersey, the Southern Tier Line, Buffalo Line, and Conrail's highly prized Chicago Line west of Cleveland to Chicago. One of the more complex arrangements was the creation of the Conrail Shared Assets Organization, which operated joint terminals in the North Jersey Terminal Area, the Philadelphia/South Jersey area, and Detroit. This essentially allowed CSX and NS to reach important customers without the need for controversial trackage rights arrangements.

During the remainder of 1997 and into 1998, NS, CSX, and Conrail carefully planned for the great division of assets and addressed the needs of communities, shippers, labor unions, and other railroads affected by the split. Numerous arrangements

were made to address specific concerns, including settlements with shippers to provide oversight of the merger process, required labor agreements, computer systems to be in place before the spilt, and CSX agreed to lower the number of trains moving through the south side of Cleveland.

The Surface Transportation Board gave verbal approval to CSX and Norfolk Southern for their acquisition and division of Conrail on June 8, 1998. In the September 1998 issue of *TRAINS Magazine*, Surface Transportation board Vice Chairman Gus Owen stated, "This merger, as approved and conditioned, approximates as closely as possible what was envisioned as far back as the [USRA's] final system plan for viable two-carrier competition in the East."

Formal written approval for the merger and division was given on July 23, 1998, and contained the board's conditions and concessions granted to other carriers. One significant condition of the merger was the imposition of a detailed service-monitoring measure to guarantee the Conrail split would not suffer from the level of operational meltdown, and consequential service disruption that occurred following the Union Pacific's takeover of Southern Pacific in 1996. On August 22, 1998, NS and CSX could exert operational control on Conrail.

However, as of that date, CSX and NS had not yet agreed on the date to spilt Conrail. They continued to work out details and build new connections to facilitate operations over Conrail Lines with their existing routes. On June 1, 1999, independent Conrail operations came to an end. Conrail still exists as a stock company and CSX and NS are the sole owners. The Conrail stock company leases assets such as locomotives and freight cars to CSX under the NYC name, and to NS under the PRR name—which reflects the heritage of the parts of Conrail that CSX and NS operate respectively. NS and CSX own Conrail stock and split the assets under leases to save huge outright acquisition tax payments. Conrail still lives in the Conrail Shared Assets Organization. In virtually all other respects, railroad operations reflect the name, paint, and style of its respective owners.

# CHAPTER FIVE

# ALONG THE OLD CANAL THE ALBANY DIVISION

## *Albany Division*

Conrail created the Albany Division in June 1987, by melding its New England and Mohawk & Hudson divisions. Its operational and administrative head-quarters were located at the sprawling Selkirk Yards south of Albany. By January 1989, the Buffalo Division and Southern Tier District were consolidated under the Albany Division's administration. At this time, the Albany Division was one of the six newly created large divisions that comprised Conrail in its final decade. Under this arrangement, the other five divisions were Dearborn, Harrisburg, Pittsburgh, Philadelphia, and Indianapolis. The consolidations of smaller regional dispatching offices coincided with administrative changes. The Albany division closed

For 15 years, Conrail routinely assigned its unique fleet of C30-7As (numbered 6550 to 6599) to Boston Line trains. Built by General Electric in 1984, the 50 C30-7As were unusual because they were six-motor locomotives powered by a 12-cylinder FDL engine instead of the standard 16-cylinder model. In October 1996, Conrail 6577 leads TV9 (Boston-Chicago) westward up Washington Hill at milepost 130 near Middlefield, Massachusetees. *Brian Solomon*

On December 9, 1984, Conrail SLSE (East St. Louis to Selkirk) rolls eastward and passes the derelict ruins of New York Central's magnificent Buffalo Terminal. Designed by architects Fellheimer & Wagner, Buffalo Terminal was opened on the eve of the Great Depression and has symbolized America's railroads fall from grace. In 1984, several active interlocking towers were still active in Buffalo. *Doug Eisele*

traditional dispatch offices at Springfield, Massachusetts, and Buffalo and Hornell, New York. Their functions were centralized at a modern new facility in Selkirk.

The Albany Division controlled former New York Central routes between New York City and Buffalo, Boston and Albany, and the Southern Tier of New York, which primarily consisted of the former Erie Railroad mainline and Buffalo.

## NEW YORK CENTRAL'S MODERN MAINLINES

In the steam era, Central's New York to Chicago Water Level Route was a heavily traveled, four-track mainline. Looking at the east-west line from Albany to Buffalo, the north tracks 3 and 4 were primarily used for slow-moving freight, while the south tracks 1 and 2 were reserved for passenger trains and fast freight such as New York Central's *Pacemaker*.

In 1927, New York Central was the first railroad to implement CTC. This precedent-setting installation was on its Ohio Division between Stanley and Berwick. CTC is a system of rules that govern the movement of trains. Under CTC rules, signals perform two distinct functions: safety protection and train control. CTC gives an operator the ability to direct train movements remotely over a long section of railroad. With CTC signaling, one operator can do more work. Controlling signals remotely over great distances allowed for the consolidation of interlocking towers. CTC has closed many line-side towers and block stations and provided a more flexible use of mainlines.

The earliest CTC installations were implemented to increase track capacity. As traffic levels dropped after World War II, railroads used CTC systems to consolidate trackage and reduce lines with traditional directional double-track to single-track operation.

The former New York Central Water Level Route was characterized by its heavy mainline, solid signal bridges, and multiple-tier telegraph poles. At 2:07 p.m. on January 12, 1986, a westbound freight approaches the interlocking at Hoffmans, New York, a few miles east of Amsterdam where the original mainline to Albany and Grand Central joined the freight main from Selkirk. *Brian Solomon*

New York Central was one of the pioneers in track reduction. In the late 1940s, it consolidated tracks between Buffalo and Cleveland and reduced its traditional four-track main to two tracks that utilized CTC.

In the mid-1950s, Central cut its New York West Shore & Buffalo Line (West Shore) to a through route west of Utica. Gradually, much of the parallel West Shore Line was abandoned. Between 1960 and 1965, Central rationalized its mainline between Albany and Buffalo and installed a modern bidirectional CTC signaling system similar to the one west of Buffalo.

Central's President Al Perlman believed technological improvements promoted efficient operations. He used CTC to increase efficiency and remove redundant tracks and plant. This saved maintenance and lowered costs. The November 1960 issue of *Modern Railroads* explained how Central's $42.5 million modernization effort between Chicago and New York used CTC signaling to operate trains in both directions on either track to give the increased operational flexibility of a double-track line. This system permitted operators to use double track to route faster

In 1986, Conrail began to rationalize the Boston Line and replace the traditional directional double with a modern single-track system with long passing sidings under the control of a Centralized Traffic Control (CTC) system. Intermediate wayside side signals were eliminated in favor of cab signals. A year after Conrail cut in the new system between Palmer and Springfield, Massachusetts, its westward PWSE (Providence & Worcester to Selkirk) departs Palmer with a cut of interchange from the Central Vermont Railway at the front of the train. The ties from the abandoned westward mainline have yet to be removed. *Brian Solomon*

trains around slower ones traveling in the same direction.

Perlman's streamlining philosophy was carried over to Conrail by former New York Central managers. New York Central's modern CTC-controlled mainlines were a stark contrast to the traditional directional double (and multiple track) mainlines of Pennsylvania Railroad. Where New York Central had closed many interlocking towers in the 1950s and 1960s, most former PRR lines continued to operate by traditional control systems well into the Conrail era. Manned towers have many operational benefits, but they can be substantially more expensive to operate. The economics of modern railroading has dictated consolidation of track control to central locations, which has resulted in labor savings. Where lines ran parallel, Conrail managers often preferred New York Central's modernized routes over PRR's traditionally operated ones.

In addition, Conrail followed the New York Central example by streamlining and modernizing many routes that suffered from over-capacity, antiquated, or inflexible trackage arrangements, and large numbers of locally manned interlocking towers.

Traditionally, directional double track is well suited to intensive passenger operations where tight scheduling is an important consideration. However, it is not as important for modern freight operations since freight traffic tends not to be as tightly scheduled. Freight only needs to meet delivery times at terminals and doesn't have to maintain minute-to-minute times between stations. Minor delays that incur while freights wait to meet each other on single-track are not a significant concern. One formula often cited to justify the conversion of directional double-track to single-track CTC states that a single-track CTC line has 75 percent of the capacity of directional double track. (In Conrail terms, centralized traffic control was known as traffic control system [TCS]. Since CTC is the more common term, this text refers to Conrail's

TCS projects as CTC to avoid confusion.) Some of this philosophy was a result of Crane's experience on Southern to Conrail. Between the 1950s and 1970s, Southern had developed a first-class, single-track mainline network with well-positioned, signalized passing sidings to allow efficient operation.

Although streamlining plant seemed necessary to lower operating costs through labor and maintenance reductions, this form of modernization is not without drawbacks. For example, Chicago-line capacity reduction was tailored to meet New York Central's later traffic demands in an era of declining passenger business, and for the most part, was adequate for Conrail traffic needs. However, the double-track arrangement placed constraints on Amtrak's desire to run significantly faster passenger trains, and was a consideration to limit passenger-train top speeds to 79 miles per hour on jointly used lines.

There are other drawbacks. Modern CTC allows a remote operator safe control of more territory, but when pushed to its limits, the effect can be counterproductive. There are limits to the performance capabilities of a single operator. In heavy or complex traffic situations, remote centralized control may impede the flow of traffic instead of expediting it, especially when extreme circumstances present unanticipated events. An experienced onsite tower operator may be able to expedite the movement of trains through an interlocking faster than a remote CTC, albeit at greater cost. In August 2003, CSX experienced a major systemwide service disruption when a computer virus disabled the centralized dispatch center and stopped the railroad.

Remote computerized CTC has made operations abstract. The operator does not see the trains, and the personal connection has been severed. This also leads to safety considerations. Traditionally, a tower operator watched each passing train roll by and looked for defects or unusual conditions that might cause an accident. Today, with an absence of people along the railroad, automated defect detectors are used to search for hot boxes (overheating journal bearings), dragging equipment, and high or wide loads. While these modern devices have prevented many wrecks, one wonders how many problems may have been avoided by having attentive, experienced railroaders trackside to observe train movements.

## HUDSON LINE

The Hudson Line is the former New York Central & Hudson River Railroad between Grand Central Terminal and Albany. From 1976 to 1982, Conrail operated commuter trains under contract with the Metropolitan Transportation Authority (MTA). In conjunction with former New Haven services, the Grand Central commuter operation was one of Conrail's most intensive operations and involved hundreds of electric and diesel-powered trains daily. Diesel trains were hauled by the fleet of former New Haven Railroad FL9 dual-mode, diesel-electric/electrics that could operate from a 16-cylinder, 567-series diesel or draw current from the line-side third rail. Heavy maintenance for the FL9 fleet and Hudson Line electric multiple units was performed at the former New York Central Harmon shops.

Conrail exited this commuter business on January 1, 1983, as New York state created the Metro North Commuter Railroad to operate the MTA commuter trains out of Grand Central Terminal. In conjunction with this transfer, Conrail conveyed its FL9 fleet and other locomotives to Metro-North.

Three four-motor GEs, led by B23-7 1925, led a coal train east on the Hudson Line between Peekskill and Roa Hook in June 1989. Conrail operated a specialized fleet of GEs with plow profiles cut to conform to the third rail in the New York electrified territory. *Brian Solomon*

Conrail continued to provide freight services over Metro-North Lines using trackage rights and retained ownership of the line north of Poughkeepsie.

Although New York City had once been a major manufacturing center, the high cost of doing business there resulted in a exodus of traditional industries. By the 1970s, very little freight traffic originated in New York City. Hudson Line traffic consisted largely of inbound shipments and interchange for the Long Island Rail Road (LIRR) (whose freight operations were privatized by the new regional railroad New York and Atlantic, which took over LIRR's freight operations in 1997). Conrail traffic was just a smattering of business compared to the high volume of business moved over this route during the peak of the New York Central era.

Conrail freight operations into New York City were based out of Hunts Point Yard in the Bronx and fed by daily trains from Selkirk. Conrail's Hudson line freight operations were largely nocturnal to avoid interference with commuter trains, as well as Metro North's daytime prohibition of trains longer than 60 cars.

The former New York Central Harlem Line once connected New York City with Chatham, an important junction with the Boston & Albany and Rutland. The line was cut as a through route in 1972, and primarily served as a commuter route to North White Plains, Brewster, and Dover Plains, New York. In later years, the freight-only business was handled by Conrail locals. In 1992, the Housatonic Railroad assumed the rights to serve Harlem Line freight customers.

## SELKIRK AND CASTLETON CUTOFF

To the unaware, the town of Selkirk near Albany seems like a sleepy village off the New York State Thruway. Selkirk Yard, which served as Conrail's largest classification yard on the Albany Division, is located in Selkirk. The yard is strategically located at the convergence of several key routes and is used to sort traffic moving across the Northeast.

Historically, New York Central's component, the West Shore, had a moderately sized freight yard at Ravenna, which is south of Selkirk. In the early 1920s, New York Central embarked on a massive plan to improve its freight operations in the Capital District. Steep grades on West Albany Hill hampered operations and required helpers on some passenger trains and most westward freight. To eliminate a bottleneck and separate the movements of freight and passenger traffic, New York Central constructed the Castleton Cutoff. This new route consisted of a branch from the Boston & Albany at Post Road to a new junction with the West Shore Albany

A westbound mixed freight from the Boston Line (the former Boston & Albany) arrives at Selkirk Yard. Three C32-8s and a C30-7A is leading the train. This freight is using a grade separated line that facilitated moves in and out of the yard. *Brian Solomon*

Branch at Selkirk. The most impressive engineering achievement is the enormous 150-foot-high, double-track bridge that carries the railroad a mile across the Hudson Valley. The Alfred H. Smith bridge was named in honor of the visionary behind the project who died prior to its completion. A low-grade connector was built to allow trains from the Hudson Line to cross the new bridge. West of Selkirk, Central upgraded its West Shore line to Rotterdam Junction (a connection with the Boston & Maine), and across the river to a junction with its Mohawk Division at Hoffmans, to allow freight to either rejoin the Water Level Route or continue west on the West Shore. New York Central had used the double-track West Shore Line as an alternate freight route to Buffalo.

An all-new yard was built at Selkirk near the new junction between the Castleton Cutoff and West Shore routes. In the Conrail era, this junction was designated CPSK. The old West Shore routes to New Jersey and Albany diverge here. The latter route served as Conrail's connection to Delaware & Hudson.

In 1968, Selkirk Yard was completely rebuilt and modernized with a computer-controlled hump yard. Conrail inherited this facility in 1976. The 1,250-acre yard stretches nearly six miles. The classification yard alone consists of 70 tracks and has a capacity of approximately 3,600 freight cars. The entire yard has an 8,500 car capacity. In the mid-1990s, Conrail classified more than 2,000 cars daily here, and dozens of freight trains originated and terminated at Selkirk Yard.

At the end of May 1999, Conrail begins its last weekend as an independent operation as freight SEAL (Selkirk to Allentown) departs Selkirk yard for its trip southward via the River Line and westward Lehigh Line. By the following Tuesday, everything in this view would be a CSX operation. *Tim Doherty*

Conrail U23Cs sit at the Selkirk fuel pad in the morning sun. The U23Cs were the last six-motor General Electric Universal-line locomotives on Conrail and outlasted all other six-motor 'U-boat' models by more than a decade. They were primarily confined to yard work at Selkirk and other large yards. *Brian Solomon*

Through freights traveled in every direction from Selkirk: down the old West Shore (known to Conrail as the River Line and part of the Philadelphia Division) 128 miles toward northern New Jersey; eastward on the Boston Line; down the Hudson Line to New York City; west to Buffalo via Hoffmans on the Water Level Route; and to Boston & Maine and Delaware & Hudson connections. In the May 1998 issue of *RailNews*, it was estimated that as many 50 to 60 freights passed through Selkirk daily.

Most manifest (mixed freight trains) serving the northeastern region originated or terminated at Selkirk. These trains used the SE designation as part of their train symbol; SEBO originated at Selkirk and terminated in Boston, and its westward counterpart was designated BOSE.

Some of the more unusual locomotives found at Selkirk were SD38s paired with yard slugs (rebuilt from six-motor Alco RSD12s, used to apply additional tractive effort) assigned to hump service. They would shove long strings of cars over the 3.5 percent-grade classification hump. Cars would roll down into the classification yard, their progress carefully braked by mechanical retarders that gripped the wheels. General Electric U23Cs were used as trimmers to assemble the cuts of cars into trains for the departure yard. These Penn Central-era locomotives were retired in the mid-1990s and replaced by C30-7As.

In addition to classification yards, Selkirk was the location of a major locomotive servicing facility, and many locomotives used on the Albany Division were serviced there. The fuel pad, where the locomotives were serviced, was populated with a variety of Conrail locomotives. It was common, especially in later years, to find a mix of off-line locomotives that ran through from western connections.

During the recession of the early 1980s, hundreds of inactive locomotives were stored at Selkirk. Storage lines ran for miles on either side of the yard and featured derelict GE U25Bs, EMD switchers, GP9s, and Alco Centuries. Some wore fading Conrail Blue, and others still carried the paint of the predecessors.

Conrail's Chicago Line begins at CP142 at Rensselaer, New York, opposite the Hudson River from Albany. This line is the natural extension of the Hudson Line, and mileposts on the route are measured from New York's Grand Central Terminal. Between Rensselaer, Schenectady, and Hoffmans, the line is a high-speed, single-tracked railroad primarily used by Amtrak's Empire Corridor trains. Through freights use the Castleton Cutoff routes.

Conrail operated local freights to industries and West Albany Yards. Prior to the construction of Selkirk in the 1920s, New York Central's West Albany Yards had been the primary classification facility in the Albany area.

West of Schenectady, the route follows the broad Mohawk River Valley across central New York state. Hoffmans is the location of a flying (grade-separated) junction where the freight line from Selkirk joins the Chicago Line.

To the west of Hoffmans, the mainline passes through Amsterdam, Fonda, Palatine Bridge, Little Falls, and Herkimer before it reaches Utica. Utica was once a significant railroad junction where the former New York Central St. Lawrence Division diverged to the north. In 1991, Conrail sold this trackage to the Mohawk, Adirondack & Northern Railroad. The company later acquired switching rights for the nearby Rome industries.

## SYRACUSE

Syracuse is the largest city in central New York. It prospered with the creation of the Erie Canal in the 1820s, and benefited from the arrival of New York Central's predecessors in the 1840s. New York Central's original mainline ran through the city streets, but in the 1930s, the tracks were relocated north of the city to improve operations and ease street congestion. The sprawling Dewitt Yards are east of downtown Syracuse, and had served as

The locomotive set for Conrail's WASE-81, led by U23B 2773, runs around its train at the Mohawk River Bridge west of Rotterdam Junction, New York, on June 10, 1989. This local carried interchange traffic for Guilford and ran between Selkirk to the yard in Rotterdam Junction. The westward facing connection between Guilford's Boston & Maine line and Conrail's line from Selkirk required locomotives to run around when delivering or collecting interchange from Selkirk. By 1990, most of the interchange to Guilford had been shifted to the Worcester, Massachusetts, gateway. *Brian Solomon*

Four General Electric B23-7s/U23Bs lead a westward freight in Lincoln Park, west of Rochester, New York, at 10:24 a.m. on December 13, 1987. Conrail's Chicago Line, the former New York Central Water Level Route, was one its most heavily traveled thoroughfares. It often hosted 40 or more through freights daily. *Brian Solomon*

one of New York Central's largest classification yards and a major locomotive shop. It once featured a double hump with a combined capacity of more than 10,000 cars. As with many traditional facilities, the classification yards and shops were downgraded and phased out in the Conrail era. The Dewitt facility was redeveloped as the site of a regional intermodal hub, which opened on September 17, 1993.

Operationally, the intermodal played an important role in allowing blocks of cars to

The Water Level Route is never quiet for long. At 9:03 a.m. on Easter Sunday 1987, an eastward double-stack lead by C36-7 6637 passes beneath the 384 signal bridge east of Churchville, New York. This was once New York Central's famous four-track mainline. The C36-7 was a 3,600 horsepower model built by General Electric and was one of the most powerful locomotives on the market at the time of its purchase in the mid-1980s. *Brian Solomon*

shift between different intermodal trains to serve different destinations. Among other tasks, this facility is used to fillet double-stack containers to single level cars for low clearance lines, such as container trains destined to Boston. The terminal features two tracks capable of handling 32 intermodal cars. A pair of overhead cranes are employed to move containers.

Syracuse is also the junction with the Montreal Secondary, a former New York Central route that runs north to Canada. In 1992, Conrail shifted its Canadian National (CN) interchange away from traditional New England gateways (Central Vermont Railway and Boston & Maine) and introduced through SECN/CNSE freights between Selkirk and Montreal. This new train often operated with through CN locomotives to Selkirk. The Chicago Line in Syracuse also connects with the New York Susquehanna & Western's former Erie Lackawanna Line to Binghamton, the former NYC Auburn Branch to Geneva, New York, and lines to Oswego, New York.

Between Syracuse and Rochester, the Chicago Line passes through wildlife refuges, rolling farmland, and the villages of Clyde, Lyons, Newark, and Palmyra. It closely follows the modern-day New York Barge Canal. A small yard is located at Lyons where the Corning Secondary (discussed below) joins the Chicago Line.

## ROCHESTER

Rochester has long been an important city along the Water Level Route. Its large population and heavy industrial base has made it a significant traffic source. It is the headquarters of Eastman Kodak, Xerox, and other major companies. Until the 1960s, Rochester was served by five railroads, but Penn Central and Conrail consolidations reduced the number of operators to two freight carriers. The most significant operation is the Water Level Route. Conrail's primary freight facility was Goodman Street Yard, which was located a

few blocks east of downtown. Its intermodal terminal was closed briefly when Conrail focused its regional intermodal services at Dewitt in 1992. It was reopened two years later as a RoadRailer facility when Conrail and Norfolk Southern formed their Triple Crown intermodal partnership.

An interesting element of the Rochester-area operation was one of the few sections of the West Shore Line west of Hoffmans that was retained by New York Central and operated by Conrail. The West Shore Branch was located between Fairport and Chili Junction and provided an alternate route to the busy Chicago Line around Rochester. Despite consolidation and elimination of redundant routes elsewhere, Conrail remained committed to this line, and rehabilitated it in the late 1980s and raised track speeds. Genesee Junction Yard served local freight traffic. A Conrail local worked the West Shore Branch and former Erie Rochester Division south to Avon where traffic was interchanged with shortline Livonia, Avon & Lakeville (LA&L). In the 1990s, the LA&L expanded its operations and acquired the Erie Line and the rights to operate into Genesee Junction along with related trackage.

The Chicago Line ascends the Niagara Escarpment west of Rochester via the Byron Hill, one of the few grades on the Water Level Route. Although Byron Hill is not especially steep, it would slow a heavy westbound to a crawl because many trains were powered for level track.

## BUFFALO

Situated on the eastern shore of Lake Erie, Buffalo had once been one of the most important industrial and transport gateways in New York state. Lines converged on Buffalo from more than a dozen directions. Competing routes, multiple yards, and a host of local industries resulted in a spider-web track that crisscrossed the city.

The creation of Conrail minimized Buffalo's importance as an interchange gate-

Conrail's ENBU (Enola to Buffalo, via the Buffalo Line) crosses the River Bridge draw in Buffalo on the former New York Central mainline on September 4, 1983. In 1984, Conrail improved its traffic flow through Buffalo by rehabilitating and incorporating the former Buffalo Creek Railroad line as its mainline. The old mainline seen here was retained as an overflow route now known as the Compromise Branch. Several interlocking towers were closed in as part of the rerouting. *Doug Eisele*

Conrail was about men and machines. Barry was an engineer on the Buffalo Division who learned the intricacies of the Boston line in the late 1980s. *Brian Solomon*

way between Eastern carriers, the Nickel Plate/Norfolk & Western and the Canadian railroads. Subsequent line and yard consolidation quieted the din of switching activity. Heavy industry that once thrived in Buffalo declined sharply during the 1970s and 1980s. Despite these changes, Buffalo remained an operational hub and was busy with through traffic.

Conrail's primary Buffalo facility was the former NYC Frontier Yard, located several miles east of downtown, and constructed by the New York Central in 1957. This was a large classification yard. Most through trains stopped for a crew change along the adjacent main tracks. The Bison Yard was located near the Frontier Yard. The modern Bison Yard didn't have a role in Conrail's greater traffic scheme and was vacated by Conrail in early 1983. NS was the yard's tenant for two more months before it was closed completely. NS returned to Bison a few years later to operate a small intermodal facility at the west end.

The New York Central mainline followed a circuitous route through Buffalo, where it faced an especially sharp, restrictive curve. In the early 1980s, Conrail improved its operations through Buffalo by converting the straighter former Buffalo Creek route to be used as its mainline while keeping one track of the traditional New York Central mainline open as the Compromise Branch for a relief valve. In the process, it closed several towers and converted operation to CTC. While this simplified operations, one drawback to the new arrangement was the creation of an operational choke point at CP DRAW. The parallel NS drawbridge was abandoned when tracks were realigned. At CP Draw, Conrail, NS, D&H, and CSX needed to gain access to nearby yards, and converged to cross the drawbridge, which created long waits during peak traffic times.

Seneca Yard, west of Buffalo, accommodated local business from Bethlehem Steel and auto parts traffic to a Ford Plant at Blasdell, New York. The western limit of the Albany Division was at Bay View, the location of Bay View interlocking tower that housed an automated high-car detector until its demolition in 1995.

## CHICAGO LINE OPERATIONS

Over its 24-year tenure, Conrail's Chicago Line operations evolved and changed greatly, but some basic traffic patterns remained consistent. As a primary route for high-priority intermodal traffic to and from East Coast cities and ports, trains needed to conform to loading schedules. Westbound intermodal trains were loaded in the evening and departed the terminals in Massachusetts and North Jersey early in the morning. They usually reached the Chicago Line by midday and raced westward every weekday afternoon. Eastbound intermodal trains needed to meet early morning arrival times at these same terminals for prompt daytime delivery to customers. Conrail often organized lower-priority schedules and slower-moving mixed freights to avoid delaying faster-moving intermodal trains. Double-track CTC on the Chicago

Line allowed Conrail dispatchers to route faster-moving intermodal trains and Amtrak trains around slower freights to minimize delays and maximize use of the track.

## NIAGARA FALLS

Conrail's predecessors in the Buffalo area operated their own branches between Buffalo and Niagara Falls. Conrail consolidated operations onto the former New York Central multiple-track Niagara branch route. This line served industries and provided a route for interchange traffic to Canada. Conrail interchanged with Canadian National via the international bridge between Black Rock, New York, and Fort Erie, Ontario. In later years, the interchange between the two railroads traveled over Conrail tracks to Frontier Yard with through CN locomotives and crews. Two bridges across the Niagara Gorge are located in Niagara Falls, as well as several yards and a junction at Tuscarora with the Falls Road to the east. The Canadian Pacific–Conrail interchange was performed here via the Toronto, Hamilton & Buffalo Route.

The Falls Road once provided a through route between Rochester and Niagara Falls, but through trains were pulled off in 1981 when Conrail scaled back operations on the Canada Southern Route. In the mid-1990s, Conrail conveyed a portion of the Falls Road between Lockport and Brockport to the shortline operator Genesee Valley Transportation's Falls Road Railroad.

Conrail's Canada Southern (CASO) Route was a 227-mile-long former New York Central double-track line across Ontario between Niagara Falls and Detroit. Traditionally, New York Central and Penn Central routed through freight and passenger traffic via Ontario, but the line did not play into Conrail's long-term plans. By the early 1980s, all through traffic had been diverted off the CASO, and only local business remained. In the mid-1980s, the line was sold to CN and CP. Evidence of Conrail's brief presence on the line remained as late as

2000, when faded Conrail-blue signs could still be seen on the old divisional headquarters at St. Thomas, Ontario.

## CORNING SECONDARY

The Corning Secondary was the old Fallbrook Line that reached south through Corning to Newberry Junction near Jersey Shore, Pennsylvania. This gave New York Central access to Pennsylvania coal country, where it operated a network of coal branches in competition with PRR. For a dozen years, Conrail operated the Corning Secondary as a through route and ran tri-weekly mixed freights between Enola and Dewitt (ENSY/SYEN), as well as unit coal trains that originated at mines in central Pennsylvania.

In 1988, Conrail abandoned the line south of Wellsboro, Pennsylvania, and lifted the tracks through the scenic "Grand Canyon of Pennsylvania," which shifted ENSY/SYEN and coal traffic to the Buffalo Line, a roughly parallel route. Between Lyons and Corning, the Corning Secondary retained sufficient local business to keep the line open. In 1995,

local operations of this line and connecting branches were conveyed to the Finger Lakes Railroad. Conrail retained ownership of the tracks and maintained trackage rights to serve the coal-fired power plant at Dresden, New York. The shortline company Wellsboro & Corning assumed operation of the remaining trackage geographically south of Corning in the early 1990s.

## BOSTON LINE

The Boston & Albany (B&A) was formed in 1867 by the merger of the Boston & Worcester and Western Railroad (of Massachusetts). The line crossed three significant grades. Charlton Hill's summit is 57 miles west of Boston. Beyond the Connecticut River crossing at Springfield is the most significant grade, Washington Hill, which crests the Berkshires 138 miles from Boston at an elevation of 1,459 feet above sea level. The railroad also crosses Richmond Summit west of Pittsfield.

As the first through railroad across southern New England from Boston to

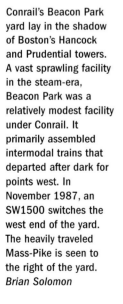

Conrail's Beacon Park yard lay in the shadow of Boston's Hancock and Prudential towers. A vast sprawling facility in the steam-era, Beacon Park was a relatively modest facility under Conrail. It primarily assembled intermodal trains that departed after dark for points west. In November 1987, an SW1500 switches the west end of the yard. The heavily traveled Mass-Pike is seen to the right of the yard. *Brian Solomon*

Conrail's SD80MACs were assigned to Boston Line in 1996. A pair of 5,000 horsepower SD80MACs intended to replace four 3,000 horsepower General Electric C30-7As. The SD80MACs used sophisticated electronics to manage three-phase alternating current motors that provided a greater tractive effort than traditional direct current motors. However, even these state-of-the-art locomotives struggled over the Boston Line's difficult profile. On this day in October 1998, it took more than 90 minutes for FRSE (Framingham, Massachusetts, to Selkirk, New York) to run 40 miles between West Springfield and the 1,459-foot summit of Washington Hill. *Tim Doherty*

points west, the B&A Route enjoyed a four-decade monopoly on freight and passenger traffic. By the later decades of the nineteenth century, the Boston & Albany was one of the most prosperous railroads in the region. In addition to a robust freight business, it developed intensive suburban traffic in the Boston area. B&A was a leader in railroad safety and was one of the first railroads to install automatic block signals.

In 1900, New York Central leased the B&A and its branches, and implemented numerous improvements to the B&A. It reduced the curve on the steepest portion of Washington Hill, bored a second State Line Tunnel portal, and constructed the Castleton Cutoff, which greatly improved the movement of freight traffic.

Despite the long decline of New England's heavy industry that began in the 1920s, the Boston & Albany suffered less from freight traffic losses than other New England gateways. The line also did not display the same degree of deterioration and decay exhibited by other northeastern routes in the late 1960s and early 1970s.

The formation of Penn Central shifted through traffic from New Haven lines to the former Boston & Albany. Since Penn Central was the only Conrail component in New England, the creation of Conrail did not result in radical changes to Boston & Albany operations.

Under Conrail, the route was designated the Boston Line, although many railroaders and observers continued to call the line the B&A. Conrail's primary yards on the Boston Line were at Beacon Park in Boston, Worcester (mainly intermodal facilities), and

West Springfield, Massachusetts. Smaller yards for local work were located in Framingham, Westboro, Palmer, and Pittsfield.

Big changes were made to the Boston Line in the 1980s as Conrail curbed operating expenses and streamlined operations. The east slope of Washington Hill has a sinuous ascent with a 1.67 percent ruling grade westbound. The tight curvature isn't as steep as some grades, but it had long presented a significant operating challenge. Traditionally,

B&A freights used helpers to assist in the climb over Washington Hill. In the late steam era, a Mikado-type locomotive would push from Chester to Washington Station, and in the Conrail era, a single six-motor unit provided typical helper power. Conrail abolished regular helper operations in 1981 and required all freights to be adequately powered for the Washington Hill ascent.

More significant changes came in 1985 following the retirement of longtime

Superintendent Ernie Cross. In October of that year, Conrail initiated its Boston Line rationalization plan. First, limited-speed crossovers were installed at key locations to prepare for the new operation by CTC. Over the next three years, the Boston Line was converted from traditional directional double-track with line-side General Railway Signal automatic block signals, to a largely single main track route under the CTC. This included a modern cab signal system that was used instead of intermediate wayside signals. With the new system, line-side signals were only used at dispatcher control points (usually designated by the initials CP followed by a milepost location). The new system was put in place between Westboro (CP33) and Selkirk Yard. The Selkirk Branch freight line between Post Road and CPSK had been converted to single-track operation many years earlier. Unlike more common single-track CTC installations, the Boston Line employed infrequent, but exceptionally long, sidings designed for limited-speed operation. Bi-directional double track was used at choke points such as Springfield and the Washington Hill where greater operational flexibility was required to keep trains moving.

In the early days, the new system did not function as well as intended. Occasionally, cab signal failures resulted in temporary placement of traditional operators stationed track-side at control points to keep trains moving. With the introduction of the Northeast Operation Rules Advisory Committee (NORAC) rules in 1988, dispatchers issued verbal authority using the Form D system. This allowed dispatchers to convey instructions directly to train crews by radio.

A program to increase the vertical clearances on the line to 19 feet as far as Westboro coincided with the single tracking and resignalling. This permitted the movement of covered multilevel autoracks and double stacks, which are taller than conventional freight cars. The large number of

After 1990, Conrail interchanged though traffic to Guilford via the Worcester, Massachusetts, gateway. LASE (Lawrence, Massachusetts, to Selkirk, New York) was one of several daily freights from Guilford. It is passing through State Line Tunnel near Canaan, New York, in May 1999. Following the Conrail split, much of the traffic carried by SELA/LASE was redirected over Guilford rails between the Albany-area New England points. *Tim Doherty*

A pair of SD40-2s lead NHSE (New Haven to Selkirk) across the Connecticut River bridge in Windsor Locks, Connecticut, on the morning of August 13, 1987. Conrail's NHSE departed Cedar Hill Yard predawn and worked Hartford yard, before it continued to Springfield, Massachusetts. The train worked west on the Boston Line midday, and arrived at Selkirk in the early evening. In later years, SENH/NHSE operated via a Hudson and Maybrook Line routing. *Brian Solomon*

bridges east of Framingham (milepost 22) made it costly to improve clearances all the way to Boston. Bridges were raised and lines undercut by 1989.

Clearance improvement helped facilitate another important change to Boston Line traffic, the relocation of the primary interchange with Guilford's Boston & Maine Route. In June 1989, Conrail signed an agreement with Providence & Worcester (P&W) to

allow the direct interchange between Conrail and Guilford over P&W tracks at Worcester. The Boston & Maine Line between Ayer, and the connection with P&W at Barbers in Worcester, had not been used for through traffic for a number of years. In the mid-1980s, it had largely served as a storage track for old B&M boxcars. To prepare for through service, the line was rehabilitated and Conrail operated trains SEAY/AYSE (Selkirk, New York, to Ayer, Massachusetts) via the Worcester Connection in November 1989. This was a prelude to the wholesale shift of the Guilford (B&M) interchange from Rotterdam Junction (west of Albany) to Worcester. It was implemented in 1990, and left the former Boston & Maine mainline via the Hoosac Tunnel devoid of most through traffic. For a few years, Guilford traffic, including most of the heavy unit coal trains to Bow, New Hampshire, used the B&A to Worcester. Unit coal trains required manned helpers, which normally operated from Selkirk all the way to Worcester. Increased traffic, as a result of the new Worcester gateway, and growing intermodal traffic to terminals at Worcester and Palmer (via Mass Central), plus the extension of MBTA commuter trains to Worcester, resulted in capacity problems on the single-track Boston Line. Unit coal trains resumed a B&M routing by 1994, and in the late 1990s, the state-funded restoration of double-track between Westboro and Worcester allowed an expanded commuter rail schedule.

## FORMER NEW HAVEN BRANCHES

As a function of the Northeast Corridor Improvement Program from the Conrail era, the former New Haven Railroad's most important corridor—Boston to New York via the Shoreline Route—was conveyed to Amtrak and the state of Connecticut, which controlled New Rochelle to New Haven.

From the Penn Central era, former New Haven lines primarily served as freight feeders to the Boston & Albany Route. Through freights originated and terminated at a variety of ex-New Haven Railroad yards and traversed the B&A to Selkirk Yard. In its early days, Conrail also operated some through freights between former New Haven points using trackage rights over the Shoreline, but this effectively ended with the passage of the Staggers Act and the line sales in the 1980s. Among the through train pairs that served New Haven lines were: SENH/NHSE (which variously operated by way of Hartford,

One of Conrail's more obscure lines was the former Connecticut Company street trackage in the New Haven, Connecticut, waterfront area. On March 2, 1989, a crewman attends to the points of a switch. In later years, this operation used former Reading Company SW1001s, such as the 9401 pictured here, because of tight clearances in New Haven. *Brian Solomon*

New Haven Railroad's sprawling Cedar Hill Yards were the center of its freight operations. Until 1966, two humps were active and dozens of freight were dispatched to points all across southern New England and to New Haven's connections at Maybrook and in New York City. Cedar Hill played a relatively minor role in Conrail operations. After 1980, flat switching was performed at the old yard in Montowese. Conrail EMD switcher 8621 was photographed at Cedar Hill on April 29, 1986. *Brian Solomon*

Connecticut; Springfield, Massachusetts; the B&A Route; and the former Maybrook Line to Hopewell Junction, via Beacon, New York, and up the Hudson Line); SESB/SBSE (Selkirk to South Braintree); a freight that ran as SEMB/MBSE after the mid-1980s (Selkirk to Middleboro, Massachusetts); and later as SERE/RESE (Selkirk to Readville, Massachusetts).

### NEW ENGLAND LINE SALES

In 1980, the once vast Cedar Hill classification yard was reduced to a flat switching facility when Conrail closed the hump yard. The yard once boasted two humps, but New Haven Railroad closed the first hump in 1966. This was a reaction to the economic recession and a prelude to the future of New Haven lines under Conrail stewardship. In early 1981, the USRA estimated that Conrail was losing more than $41 million on its lines in New England, with little hope of improving its situation. The subsequent dismemberment of New Haven reflected the difficulties of operating New England lines profitably.

To cut its New England losses, Conrail made changes to its Connecticut branch line network in 1982. It sold potentially profitable lines to both new and existing New England

railroads. Boston & Maine took over operations of lines running to Plainville and Waterbury by a new trackage-rights arrangement between Springfield, Hartford, and Berlin. B&M was also granted limited trackage rights to Cedar Hill. In addition, B&M assumed operation of the Armory Branch, a portion of the old New York & New England that ran south from Springfield, Massachusetts, to Hazardville, Connecticut.

The Providence & Worcester began operation in 1973 over its namesake route, which was previously operated by Penn Central. As Conrail retrenched, P&W expanded and gradually pieced together much of the remaining former New Haven routes. Although P&W had other New England gateways, it fed most traffic to Conrail.

A number of new shortlines were created in New England as Conrail scaled back. Like P&W, these also fed traffic to Conrail. Selling branches typically generated more traffic from former New Haven routes than if Conrail had operated the lines itself.

Pioneer Valley was among the new lines, and it assumed operations of portions of the former Canal Line between Westfield, Holyoke, and Easthampton, Massachusetts. The Housatonic Railroad began in the mid-1980s and expanded southward over the historic route of the original Housatonic Railroad to Danbury, Connecticut, in 1992 when it purchased Conrail Danbury-area branches. In 1995, Connecticut Southern (owned by holding company Rail America) began operations and primarily provided freight service on the New Haven to Springfield line (by this time owned by Amtrak) and related branchlines. By 1995, Conrail had exited most former New Haven lines. The few remaining former New Haven branchlines in eastern Massachusetts were put on the block in 1996, but their sale was halted by the CSX/NS split of Conrail.

## SOUTHERN TIER

The Southern Tier was the largest and most significant portion of the Erie Lackawanna operated by Conrail in later years. It provided a marginally shorter route between northern New Jersey terminals and Buffalo than the former New York Central routes, but it faced a significantly more difficult profile. Since the Erie Route missed many major manufacturing centers, it had far less on-line business than the former NYC. In a January 1981 *TRAINS Magazine* article by Fred Frailey, Conrail operations chief Richard Hassleman explained, "This is beautiful scenery, of course, and the Delaware Division is lovely. But what the hell is down there? It's

Conrail 3268 leads OIBU-9 (Oak Island, New Jersey, to Buffalo, New York) through fog at Canaseraga, New York, on September 30, 1988. In 1988 and 1989, the former Erie, known as the Southern Tier, was heavily traveled with Conrail freight. At the time, Conrail was improving its River Line between Selkirk and northern New Jersey terminals, which later accommodated most through traffic that moved over the Southern Tier. *Brian Solomon*

Conrail SD40-2 6427 leads American Presidents Line TV305 as it roars westward through the Canisteo River Valley west of Rathbone, New York, near milepost 307. The Southern Tier was Conrail's initial route for transcontinental double-stack landbridge trains. Delaware & Hudson DHT9, a Sealand double-stack, often followed a Conrail APL train across the Southern Tier route. *Brian Solomon*

a perfectly adequate alternative route from New Jersey to Buffalo, but we don't have an overload via Selkirk."

It is doubtful that the old Delaware Division or the rest of the Southern Tier would have survived rounds of rationalization if New York state hadn't stepped in. The state wanted to preserve the Erie Route in order to boost the economically deprived communities along the Southern Tier. This policy had historical precedent since the Erie Railroad had been built 130 years earlier to aid the region's poor economy. The state of New York funded Conrail's rehabilitation of Erie routes,

including the Meadville Line west of Hornell in the late 1970s. In exchange for state money to upgrade the line, Conrail agreed to operate a minimum number of through trains per week over the former Erie Route and to retain the lines until at least the 1990s.

Although it was unforeseen at the time of this unusual agreement, by the mid-1980s, maintaining the Erie Route had proved fortuitous for Conrail. The Erie had much higher clearances than Conrail's other east-west mainlines. In 1984, when American President Lines organized a transcontinental land bridge for its new double-stack container

trains, Conrail's Erie Route was ideal to deliver the trains to Kearny, New Jersey. Its other mainlines suffered from low clearances that required expensive upgrading. Double-stack traffic was one of the largest growth areas in the wake of Staggers. For the duration of the 1980s, the Southern Tier Route was Conrail's preferred double-stack route. As Conrail gradually raised clearances on its other primary routes, stack traffic was diverted away from the Southern Tier. However, Conrail used the line as a diversionary route when other mainlines were blocked by derailments, closed for maintenance, or became congested with traffic.

In addition to Conrail through and local traffic, the Southern Tier hosted Delaware & Hudson (D&H) trains for 206 miles between Binghamton and Buffalo, as a result of trackage rights granted with the creation of Conrail. Over the years, D&H traffic to Buffalo ebbed and flowed to reflect economic patterns and changes in the railroad industry. D&H moved various mixed freight, intermodal, coal, and grain trains over the Southern Tier.

Beginning in 1985, D&H forwarded Sealand double-stack trains from the New York, Susquehanna & Western (NYS&W). The latter line moved the trains from its Little Ferry, New Jersey, intermodal terminal over the Delaware Division thanks to haulage rights purchased from Conrail in the early 1980s. In the late 1980s, NYS&W acquired a portion of the former Lehigh & Hudson River Route. It rebuilt this line in conjunction with a portion of its own lines to ease commuter train congestion in the New Jersey–New York suburban area.

CP Rail purchased the bankrupt Delaware & Hudson in 1991. CP Rail wanted to purchase the western portion of the Southern Tier from Conrail. However, CP and Conrail could not agree on terms of the sale, and Conrail retained the line.

Retaining the line in 1992, Conrail initiated a single-track, CTC, and track-rehabilitation program. Sections of directional double-track from Waverly to Elmira and Corning to River Junction (near Hunt, New York) were converted to a single-track line under control of CTC (Elmira–Corning had already been double-track CTC). Many miles of jointed rail were replaced with continuous welded rail, which allowed some speed increases.

Modernization resulted in the replacement of the traditional Union Switch & Signal Style-S upper quadrant semaphore, which dated back to World War I, with modern triangular-patterned, color-light signals. The line-side telegraph poles that carried codelines were also removed. Conrail never

Conrail OIEL (Oak Island, New Jersey, to Elkhart, Indiana) works the Meadville Line east of East of Andover, New York, on September 30, 1988. This line faced a stiff westward grade between Hornell and Andover. Erie built a low-grade cutoff between River Junction (on the Southern Tier) and Cuba Junction (on the Meadville Line) so heavy westward freights could avoid the climb. Conrail abandoned the cutoff in the late 1970s, demolished a huge trestle at Belfast, and forced remaining trains to cross Andover Hill. *Brian Solomon*

completed its modernization of the line, and the portion between Binghamton and Waverly retained its traditional arrangement. As of 2003, one semaphore remains near Endicott, New York.

Conrail's primary yard on the Southern Tier was at Gang Mills west of Corning.

Hornell had been the location of a large Erie railroad yard and shop complex. Although the shops were not used by Conrail, they were purchased locally and subsequently leased to a succession of companies that built and refurbished various railroad and transit equipment. One of the engineering highlights and operational difficulties of the Southern Tier is the Portageville Trestle across the Upper Falls of the Genesee River at Letchworth State Park. This ancient bridge has a maximum speed of just 10 miles per hour, and as of 2003, is under consideration for total rebuild by NS.

At Silver Springs, traffic was interchanged with Chessie System. Later, it was interchanged with Genesee & Wyoming and its sister company, Rochester & Southern, which purchased the former Baltimore & Ohio route in 1986.

Farther to the west, the Attica Hill grade presented a challenge to eastbound trains. During the 1980s, D&H assigned helpers to heavy trains between Buffalo and Warsaw.

Until the early 1980s, the Southern Tier Line ended at Bison Yard east of Buffalo. After its closure, Conrail trains continued a few miles west to join the Water Level Route at what eventually became CP DRAW. Conrail trains that moved to and from the Water Level Route often changed crews at William Street, adjacent to the Delaware and Hudson's former Conrail SK Yard in Buffalo. D&H relocated there after Bison Yard was closed.

Until 1990, Conrail routed through traffic over the Meadville Line and Southern Tier (former Erie Railroad) mainline routes. On the morning of April 20, 1989, Conrail 3205 leads ELOI (Elkhart, Indiana, to Oak Island, New Jersey) along the Canisteo River east of Rathbone, New York. This train operated over the Meadville Line via Jamestown, Salamanca, and Olean, New York to Hornell. The Meadville Line joined the Southern Tier line at Cass Street in Hornell. *Brian Solomon*

# CHAPTER SIX

# PHILADELPHIA DIVISION

Conrail's Philadelphia Division was comprised of a rainbow of its predecessors routes. Divisional boundaries reached from Selkirk, New York, in the shadow of New York's capitol, to Potomac Yard in Alexandria, Virginia, in the shadow of the nation's capitol. In Conrail's 1988 administrative consolidation, it combined the Reading and Lehigh Divisions into a much-enlarged Philadelphia Division. With this enlargement, in addition to former Reading and Lehigh Valley routes, the Philadelphia Division trackage consisted of the former New York Central West Shore Route between Weehawken, New Jersey, and Selkirk, New York, plus former Pennsylvania Railroad lines in New Jersey and eastern Pennsylvania, including trackage rights on Amtrak's Northeast Corridor. In 1995, the Philadelphia Division incorporated portions of the Harrisburg Division, including the southern part of the Buffalo Line.

The typical traffic pattern on Conrail's River Line normally resulted in westward double-stack traffic traversing the line in darkness. On July 1, 1998, the pattern was altered by a lightning strike that damaged a signal control cabinet, which resulted in a signal failure. This disrupted Conrail's normally predictable operation on the River Line and permitted an atypical early morning photograph of TV209 at milepost 44 near Ft. Montgomery. TV209 carried double-stacks interchange with western connections in Chicago. *Tim Doherty*

The 1970s and early 1980s saw a transformation in the traffic Conrail carried in the region. As the traditional base related to heavy manufacturing in eastern Pennsylvania and New Jersey declined, new intermodal traffic grew. Outbound manufactured products gave way to imported goods from the Far East. New York City had once produced goods for the rest of the country and the world, but by the mid-Conrail era, it had become the importer of goods from elsewhere. The transformation from mixed-carload freights to solid, mile-long intermodal trains occurred gradually in Conrail's first decade. Intermodal business really took off in Conrail's second decade.

New York remained a primary gateway for shipments moving overseas. The Port of New York and New Jersey is the nation's busiest Atlantic port. The shift toward the containerization of ocean-going freight started in the 1950s, and by the 1970s, containers had become a standard in international shipping. To better accommodate intermodal shipments, the Port Authority of New York & New Jersey developed modern deepwater container port facilities in Newark and Elizabeth, New Jersey.

Conrail's primary intermodal routes converged at the port where mile-long intermodal trains arrived from points west to meet morning delivery times in the New York market, be distributed to a multitude of points in the Northeast, or transferred to ships bound for Europe and elsewhere abroad.

## WEST SHORE ROUTE

By the mid-1990s, one significant intermodal route was the former West Shore Route, known under Conrail as the River Line. It followed the Hudson River for 142 miles between Jersey City and Selkirk. This was the modern way of how the Water Level Route freight reached New York. A trickle of Gotham-bound freight traveled down the Hudson Line on the east side of the river, and the majority moved via the River Line to New Jersey terminals.

In the New York Central era, this directional double-track route was converted to a mostly single-track line under CTC with sidings every 20 miles. As Conrail traffic grew, it gradually lengthened and added sidings to allow great traffic capacity. To overcome limitations of the single-track line, Conrail would fleet trains moving in one direction.

The 10-mile stretch between Jones Point near milepost 40 to milepost 50 near the base of Storm King Mountain is the most impressive section of the River Line. The tracks hug the river bank, cross Iona Island in New York's Bear Mountain State Park, and cross three trestles. The line passes under the

Running between Selkirk and its connection with Norfolk Southern in Hagerstown, SENS passes beneath the New Jersey Turnpike in Jersey City on the afternoon of October 28, 1997. The lower Manhattan skyline is seen in the background.
*Tim Doherty*

famous Bear Mountain Bridge, which spans the Hudson, and tunnels beneath the U.S. Military Academy at West Point.

Conrail operations on the River Line were greatly improved from the days of Penn Central when miles of 10-miles-per-hour slow orders had been imposed on the line as a result of deferred maintenance. The route was one of the first rehabilitated by Conrail. In the 1990s, the transcontinental intermodel train TVLA covered the line in just 4 1/2 hours. In the late 1980s, Conrail raised clearances on the River Line to accommodate double stacks and covered multilevels. Conrail closed the line in the summer of 1988 so the West Point Tunnel could be enlarged.

## NORTH JERSEY TERMINALS

Conrail operated a complex maze of trackage in northern New Jersey that connected a multitude of yards, terminals, and port facilities. Prior to 1976, each of Conrail's component railroads had maintained its own facilities in the New York metro area. Conrail consolidated as many of these as possible.

*Top:* Conrail TV10 crosses Iona Island on its trip down River Line on July 1, 1998. This intermodal train departed Chicago the previous day and it has less than 40 miles before it reaches its terminal in North Bergen, New Jersey. Dependable early morning arrivals were a hallmark of Conrail Intermodal service to New York metropolitan area because shippers could provide same day delivery after the train arrived. *Tim Doherty*

*Above:* Conrail delivered finished automobiles to distribution points in New Jersey and at Port Newark for shipment overseas with its fleet of specialized unit auto-rack trains known as multilevels. Conrail ML480 passes milepost 40 on the River Line near Jones Point along the Hudson River in New York state. *Tim Doherty*

On July 24, 1998, Conrail's deluxe Office Car Special (OCS) traveling on the River Line crosses Popolopne Creek against a background of the Bear Mountain Bridge. The OCS is midway through a trip for Conrail's Automotive Group between Framingham, Massachusetts, and Philadelphia. Passengers on the Hudson River leg of the trip included a group of Conrail Auto terminal stevedores who were being rewarded for working 16 months without injury. *Tim Doherty*

Lehigh Valley's Oak Island Yard near Newark was retained as a classification yard and developed to serve a variety of different routes. Following an $18 million renovation in 1981, Oak Island assumed switching, which had previously been performed by the former Pennsy Waverly Yard and Central Railroad of New Jersey's Elizabethport Yard.

As intermodal traffic developed, Conrail expanded its facilities to handle the traffic. Most intermodal terminals were situated on the site's yards that were once used to accommodate carload traffic. The northernmost facility in the metro area is the former New York Central Yard in North Bergen, New Jersey, on the southern end of the River Line. This yard primarily handled piggyback trailers and was close to a UPS terminal. At the easternmost end of the Southern Tier Route was the former Erie Croxton Yard.

Eastward intermodal train symbol Mail-8 has arrived at New Jersey's South Kearny Yard and has pulled ahead over HACK Bridge in order to yard its train. This movable bridge and tower over the Hackensack River is situated between South Kearney yard on the west and the beginning of the River Line route and Northern Branch on the east. The bridge provided one of two north-south routes through the North Jersey terminal area. The other route is via Upper Bay. *Tim Doherty*

Trains traversing Conrail's River Line reached Newark-area terminals via a former PRR line that ran parallel to the PATH rapid transit system. Conrail tracks ran side-by-side with PATH for about a mile through Jersey City. Here the Allentown to Selkirk freight (ALSE) is about to traverse PATH's Journal Square Station on March 23, 1997. The Port Authority Trans-Hudson was built as PRR subsidiary Hudson & Manhattan. The rapid transit trains carried PRR keystones at one time. *Tim Doherty*

This was transformed from a carload yard to an intermodal double-stack facility. Likewise, the former Pennsy Meadows Yard at South Kearny was transformed into an intermodal yard and an American Presidents Line double-stack terminal.

To facilitate the direct movement of containers between ships and trains, an ExpressRail dockside intermodal yard was built at the sprawling Port Newark complex in Elizabeth. This opened in August 1991

Conrail rebuilt Lehigh Valley's Oak Island Yard in Newark, New Jersey. It remained a center for car-load freight operations in the New York metro area. The yard can viewed from numerous highway overpasses in this section of New Jersey. *Tim Doherty*

One of Conrail's Port Newark local freights switches cars with a General Electric DASH 8-40B (B40-8 in Conrail parlance) as a plane lands at the nearby Newark Airport. The high-horsepower B40-8s were built for Conrail in 1988 and were originally assigned to its fastest intermodal trains.*Tim Doherty*

A local led by a B23-7 1911 heads back to the yard office and passes one of Port Newark's finest dining establishments.
*Tim Doherty*

The primary objective of Conrail's police force was to protect company property. This role was especially necessary along the River Line in Hoboken where a public housing complex adjacent to the tracks provided cover for thieves who attempted to rob passing Conrail's trains. Conrail's police reacted to this persistent threat and paced every train that ran through Hoboken in their squad cars. On March 23, 1997, ALSE (Allentown to Selkirk) was guarded by no less than seven Conrail police cars in Hoboken. *Tim Doherty*

and is operated by the Port Authority of New York & New Jersey.

Another cooperative venture was the joint operation by Conrail and Norfolk Southern of a RoadRailer yard situated between the New Jersey Turnpike and Port Newark. Another intermodal yard is located near the site of the former CNJ shops at Elizabethport.

A yard at Port Reading handled traffic to New Jersey's "Chemical Coast" along the Arthur Kill waterway that separates New Jersey and Staten Island, New York. Chemical industries and refineries line the Chemical Coast Secondary from Newark to South Amboy. Auto loading and unloading yards in Newark and Little Ferry, New Jersey, would send outbound imported cars on multilevel

autorack trains to the rest of the country, and inbound autoracks would feed the distribution of cars for the New York area and for shipment overseas.

## CORRIDOR EXODUS

In its early years, Conrail moved a considerable volume of north-south freight traffic over the Northeast Corridor (NEC). In its first decade, Conrail routinely operated intermodal and manifest trains on the same tracks as Amtrak's fast passenger trains. Amtrak's trackage-rights charges were among the highest in the United States, and further pressure after the deadly collision between a set of three Conrail light engines and Amtrak's *Colonial* in Chase, Maryland, in 1987 forced Conrail to seek alternative routes.

In the 1970s, USRA's Conrail final system plan suggested alternate routes for Northeast Corridor freight traffic. One plan envisioned Conrail using parallel trackage to the corridor that consisted of Lehigh Valley, Reading, and B&O routes. This would remove freight traffic from the heavily used NEC. This plan took more than a decade to implement.

By 1986, Conrail had shifted most traffic to parallel routes. Nearly all of the through traffic was off the NEC. In 1991, Conrail shifted most Philadelphia–Baltimore–Washington traffic off the NEC to CSX's parallel Washington to Philadelphia line. Conrail had worked with CSX in the operation of successful joint services, such as the Tropicana orange juice train (ran from Bradenton, Florida, to Greenville, New Jersey); TV-173/174 intermodal trains running between Atlanta and South Kearny, New Jersey; and a daily SECS/CSSE that operated from Selkirk via the Trenton, Lehigh, and River Lines and interchanged with CSX in Philadelphia.

After 1991, a few Conrail locals were required to service customers along the

Conrail GP30s 2173 and 2246 were photographed in Baltimore, Maryland, on October 21, 1980. The GP30 uses a 16-cylinder 567D3 to produce 2,250 horsepower, which was considered high-output for a four-motor model when it was introduced by Electro-Motive in 1961. They were different from other models because of their semi-streamlined appearance. Conrail inherited GP30s from PRR, Reading, and New York Central. *Doug Eisele*

On the afternoon of October 27, 1997, Conrail ALCA (Allentown, Pennsylvania, to Camden, New Jersey) emerges from the east portal of 4,875-foot Pattenburg/Musconetcong Tunnel. In the 1980s, Conrail shifted traffic from former PRR North East Corridor routes to the Lehigh Line. By the mid-1980s, this former Lehigh Valley mainline served as a key link in Conrail's primary east-west route between the New York metro area and its former PRR Pittsburgh Line. *Tim Doherty*

NEC. Auto traffic to Ford and GM plants in Linden and Metuchen, New Jersey, remained, as did some through traffic that continued to ply the section between Wilmington, Delaware, and Baltimore.

Conrail moved traffic to Delaware and Baltimore from Enola Yard via the Port Road Secondary, which followed the Susquehanna River to Perryville, Maryland, where it met the NEC. Coal traffic to Baltimore and the automotive business to and from Newark, Delaware, were among the more important uses of the Port Road. Conrail's Baltimore-area operations were centered at the former PRR Bayview Yard, situated parallel to the NEC northeast of downtown. Conrail's export coal docks were located on the Baltimore waterfront.

Near Washington, D.C., the 10-mile-long Landover Line provided a connection between the NEC, Conrail's Benning Yard,

and Richmond, Fredricksburg & Potomac's Potomac Yard at Alexandria, Virginia, to avoid congested Washington Union Station trackage. This line also hosted CSX freights via trackage rights. The shift away from NEC's routings to CSX lines and to Norfolk Southern via the Hagerstown, Maryland, gateway, was related to downgrading and eventual closure of RF&P's Potomac Yard.

### LEHIGH AND TRENTON LINE ROUTES
The former Lehigh Valley mainline, known to Conrail as the Lehigh Line, evolved as a primary route for traffic moving to New Jersey terminals. The line begins at Oak Island and runs to Allentown, and to a connection with the Southern Tier at Waverly, New York. Port Reading Junction is 21 miles west of Oak Island and connects with the Trenton Line, the former Reading Route to Philadelphia, and CSX's former B&O

Philadelphia–Washington mainline. The Reading and B&O lines hosted B&O's famous *Royal Blue* in the passenger era. Reading and B&O used the Central Railroad of New Jersey, but Conrail used the Lehigh Valley Route.

## LEHIGH LINE

West of Port Reading Junction, the engineering highlight of the Lehigh Line is the 4,875-foot-long Pattenburg (Musconetcong) Tunnel near Bellewood, New Jersey. Between Phillipsburg, New Jersey, and Easton, Pennsylvania, the line crossed the Delaware River via the former CNJ Bridge. In the 1980s, Conrail shifted the line, rather than repair the decaying Lehigh Valley Bridge. The sprawling Bethlehem steel plant was parallel to the tracks for miles until 1995 when the

plant closed, which provided Conrail with a large volume of steel-related traffic.

At CP BETHLEHEM, a junction directed traffic to Allentown Yard across the Lehigh River, while through trains for the Reading continued via CP BURN. Lehigh Valley acquired the large Allentown classification yard from CNJ in 1972, which allowed it to consolidate and close some of its smaller yards. This facility played well into Conrail's traffic patterns, and Conrail invested $18 million to completely rebuild it.

West of CP ALLEN, the Lehigh Line continues westward to Waverly, via Lehighton, Jim Thorpe, and DuPont, Pennsylvania. Conrail traffic was relatively light west of Allentown. Trains CGAL/ALCG (Corning/Gang Mills, New York to Allentown) or BUAL/ALBU (Buffalo to Allentown) ran this line at different

A pair of light engines led by C30-7A 6562 negotiate Oxbow Bend in the Lehigh River Gorge west of Jim Thorpe, Pennsylvania, on October 22, 1991. The former Lehigh Valley mainline between Allentown and Sayre, Pennsylvania, played a nominal role in Conrail operations. *Brian Solomon*

In August 1998, a Conrail local works dockside warehouses in South Philadelphia near the *SS United States*. Commercial airlines helped kill privately operated intercity passenger trains and wrecked the Trans-Atlantic passenger ship business. The *SS United States* carried its last passengers in 1969 and has been laid up, first at Newport News, then at Philadelphia ever since. *Tim Doherty*

times. Delaware & Hudson operated on the Lehigh Line between DuPont and Newark, New Jersey. This was intended to be D&H's outlet to the New York metropolitan area, but it never produced much traffic. The route was significantly longer than the parallel Conrail lines, which made its intermodal schedules uncompetitive with Conrail's. D&H also didn't have access to most of the lucrative northern New Jersey traffic and was denied direct access to carload traffic.

In the mid-1990s, Conrail sold the Lehigh Line railroad west of Lehighton to the Reading Blue Mountain & Northern. After the sale, Conrail retained rights to serve a large Procter & Gamble plant in Mehoopany via Waverly and Sayre from its Southern Tier Line. Although the Lehigh Valley mainlines between Van Etten

Junction and Buffalo were not included in Conrail's operations, the former Lehigh Valley Line to Ithaca and Lansing, New York, was retained to serve a coal-fired power plant and salt mine.

## PHILADELPHIA

The Philadelphia-area operations were more intensive in the early Conrail years before traffic was shifted away from the former PRR Northeast Corridor routings. To Northeast Corridor charges, Conrail routed most traffic through Philadelphia with its former Reading lines. The Harrisburg Line is a former Reading route between Philadelphia, Reading, and Harrisburg, Pennsylvania, that also provides a route to Allentown. Delaware & Hudson served the Port of Philadelphia via trackage rights over this route.

At Park Junction in Philadelphia, the Trenton Line connected with CSX's former B&O mainline. This was where Conrail handed off its north-south intermodal trains, the Tropicana orange juice train, and carload mixed-freight traffic destined to CSX.

Greenwich Yard was a nerve center for Conrail's operations on Philadelphia's south side. It served coal, ore, and grain facilities, local freight, and the Delaware River Port Authority's container port served by the D&H that ran on trackage rights. In 1990, Conrail shifted export coal traffic that traditionally moved to Philadelphia, to coal terminals in Baltimore. Philadelphia remained a trans-loading point for inbound iron-ore traffic destined to Weirton Steel, U.S. Steel, and Bethlehem Steel. Other imported semi-finished steel slabs were unloaded from ships in Philadelphia to be delivered to domestic steel mills.

A Conrail Yard in Frankford Junction northeast of Philadelphia served local industry. Pavonia Yard in Camden, New Jersey, was an operational hub for the network of former Pennsylvania–Reading Seashore lines radiating across southern New Jersey. In 1996, Conrail proposed selling these lucrative routes, but the sale was cancelled because of the Conrail split.

## READING LINE AND HARRISBURG LINES

Reading, Allentown, and Bethlehem, Pennsylvania, were connected by the Reading Line. This former Reading Company corridor was once a key portion of the Alphabet Route that allowed smaller railroads to compete for through traffic with the Pennsy, New York Central, and Baltimore & Ohio under the regulated rate structure. Conrail developed portions of the old Alphabet Route as its preferred alternative to former Pennsy routes to avoid the NEC. Thus, the Reading Line was used to move traffic between Harrisburg and New Jersey, and to the Norfolk Southern via Lurgan Branch and Hagerstown. Beginning on January 1, 1987, Conrail shifted its high-priority intermodal mail trains Mail-3/4 and

Mail-8/9 to the former LV/Reading route between Harrisburg and North Jersey.

The former Reading Company Harrisburg Line is a slightly longer route between Philadelphia and Harrisburg than the parallel former Pennsy route owned by Amtrak. The Reading Line joins the Harrisburg Line at Reading, Pennsylvania. This is a mostly double-track route except for single-track sections through the tunnels near Philadelphia, Flat Rock, and Phoenixville.

The Harrisburg Line was unusual in the modern era because it was not controlled by CTC signaling. During Conrail's last couple of summers, track and signal work on the Harrisburg Line opened temporary block-control stations where operators, following instructions from the train dispatcher, manually operated crossovers and issued Form-D orders to authorize the trains' movement.

## LURGAN BRANCH

North-south traffic for interchange with CSX or Norfolk Southern that used the old Reading Company/Alphabet Route diverged from the Harrisburg Line at CP CAPITAL in Harrisburg. This traffic crossed the Susquehanna River by the former Reading bridge to reach the Lurgan Branch. It was 42 miles between CP CAPITAL and the connection with CSX at Lurgan. Interchange with NS was via the Hagerstown Secondary between Shippensburg, Pennsylvania, and Hagerstown, Maryland. In the 1980s, traffic that used this route was normally one pair of scheduled trains. Frequency was boosted when Conrail and Norfolk Southern shifted their interchange away from Potomac Yard. By 1997, traffic included six pairs of scheduled trains, including manifest, conventional intermodal, and RoadRailer trains moving to NS.

## ENOLA AND HARRISBURG

Conrail's east-west traffic continued on former Pennsy routes via CP HARRIS adjacent to the Harrisburg Amtrak Station. To alleviate a bottleneck, Conrail added a second track in the

Pennsylvania Railroad's Enola Yards were once the largest freight classification facility in the world. Under Conrail, Enola's functions were gradually transferred to other facilities, and the hump was closed in the early 1990s. This view of Enola was captured on a hazy afternoon in July 1987. *Brian Solomon*

mid-1990s. CP HARRIS is part of Amtrak's former Pennsy electrified Harrisburg line from Philadelphia. Although Amtrak's former PRR route is shorter than Conrail's former Reading lines, Conrail shifted traffic away from the Amtrak line in the 1980s to avoid high charges. Harrisburg Conrail operated a large intermodal terminal and a run-through fuel pad to service locomotives of the through trains west of CP HARRIS.

Most east-west trains that used the former PRR Pittsburgh Line crossed the Susquehanna via the Rockville Bridge (see chapter 7, The Heart of Conrail). On the west bank of the Susquehanna, south of the

bridge and opposite Harrisburg, is the vast former PRR Enola Yard. Enola was the largest freight classification yard in the world. It was Conrail's second busiest yard in the late 1970s. Enola lost importance as Conrail moved away from carload traffic and shifted trains away from former PRR routings east of Harrisburg. Yards such as Allentown to the east and Conway to the west assumed much of the work formerly done at Enola. The yard was in decline by the early 1980s, and it was shut and its hump was closed in the early 1990s. A few years later, the yard was reopened for flat switching, but it was a shadow compared to the integral role it

Conrail's Buffalo Line connected Harrisburg to Buffalo via Sunbury, Lock Haven, and Keating Summit, Pennsylvania. On a dark, damp, November 1998 afternoon, a Conrail SD60M leads a Multilevel (auto carrier) eastward toward Harrisburg railroad, east of Sunbury, Pennsylvania along the Susquehanna River. Traditional Pennsylvania Railroad position light signals give away the line's heritage. *Brian Solomon*

During a brisk autumn shower, a Conrail Multilevel train glides through Hyner, Pennsylvania, along the Buffalo Line east of Renovo, Pennsylvania. The Buffalo Line served a limited role in latter-day Conrail operations and accommodated a few trains a day. *Brian Solomon*

played during Pennsy times.

## BUFFALO LINE

Conrail's Buffalo Line was comprised of the former PRR and Northern Central line to Sunbury, the old Philadelphia & Erie route between Sunbury and Emporium, and the line via Keating Summit, Pennsylvania, and Olean, New York, to Buffalo. West of Emporium, the line faced a steep climb to Keating Summit, and helpers were routinely assigned to move heavy trains.

The Buffalo Line had been a busy route in the PRR era. Major shop facilities were located at Renovo. Under Conrail, the Buffalo Line was essentially a secondary mainline. It was used by coal trains that originated in central Pennsylvania and joined the line at Keating and Lock Haven. Other junctions were located in Emporium and Driftwood. In addition to coal traffic, considerable local traffic was generated between Sunbury and Lock Haven. Conrail operated moderately sized yards at Emporium, Williamsport, and Lock Haven. As coal traffic declined, so did the importance of these yards.

In later years, through traffic consisted of a pair of mixed freights between Buffalo and Enola, and of a pair of automotive carrying multilevel trains (ML411 & ML420) between Buffalo and facilities in Delaware. Delaware & Hudson exercised trackage rights between Sunbury and Harrisburg. The northernmost section of the line was administered by Albany Division. When Genesee & Wyoming's Buffalo & Pittsburgh abandoned its B&O route between Ashford Junction and Buffalo in the mid-1990s, B&P acquired trackage rights from Machias to Buffalo, New York, via the Conrail Buffalo Line.

In 1990s, Conrail considered rationalizing and selling portions of the Buffalo Line, and it probably would have gone through with these plans if CSX and NS hadn't split the line.

Conrail's Buffalo Line between Harrisburg and Buffalo utilized part of the old Northern Central route to Sunbury and continued west on the old Philadelphia & Erie line to Emporium, Pennsylvania, where the line climbed over Keating Summit toward Olean. On November 1, 1991, a westward Conrail train led by DASH 8-40CW 6140 negotiates streetside trackage on the Buffalo Line in downtown Sunbury, Pennsylvania. *Brian Solomon*

# CHAPTER SEVEN

# THE HEART OF CONRAIL

## *Broad Way*

**The Pennsylvania Railroad** was exemplified by its four-track artery, the famous Broad Way across central Pennsylvania. It was an east-west route that funneled traffic from around the railroad and across the nation. Under Conrail, these former PRR lines underwent a variety of changes. During its 1988 administrative restructuring, Conrail merged its Cleveland and Pittsburgh divisions. Divisional headquarters were based in the Pittsburgh suburb of Greentree. During the 1995 restructuring, western portions of the Harrisburg Division were combined with the Pittsburgh Division.

In the mid-1990s, Conrail's road fleet was augmented by DASH 8-40CWs leased by General Electric subsidiary LMS. These locomotives worked Conrail lines during peak traffic, and were leased to other railroads during the slower times of the year. LMS 724 leads a Conrail freight at Mineral Point, Pennsylvania, on September 5, 1997. *Brian Solomon*

### WEST FROM HARRISBURG

In 1834, the Commonwealth of Pennsylvania opened its "Main Line of Public Works." It was an unusual combination of transport modes that linked Philadelphia with Pittsburgh. The Main

Conrail SD40-2 6452 climbs around Horseshoe Curve at 2:14 p.m. on July 27, 1988. The famous Horseshoe Curve was engineered by PRR Chief Engineer and President J. Edgar Thomson and opened to traffic in February 1854. *Brian Solomon*

Line was a railroad, canal, and an inclined-portage railway, which employed a series of very steep (8 to 10 percent) inclined planes to move canal packet boats over the mountains. Stationary steam locomotives and cables hauled the packets up and down the grades. The boats were split in half before they were placed on the inclines' rails. The Main Line was built in response to New York state's Erie Canal and Maryland's Baltimore & Ohio Rail Road transportation systems that moved valuable traffic from the Allegheny and Niagara Frontiers, Ohio Valley, and beyond, to the ports of New York and Baltimore. The Main Line cut passenger transit time between Philadelphia and Pittsburgh from more than a week to a little more than four days. The PRR eventually purchased the Main Line from the state and integrated part of its route from Philadelphia and abandoned the rest.

The Pennsylvania Railroad was laid out by John Edgar Thomson. Born in 1808, and a civil engineer by trade, Thomson was appointed PRR's chief engineer in 1847. He was appointed president in 1852 and held the post for 20 years. Thomson built west from Harrisburg and followed the Juniata and Little Juniata Rivers west toward the Allegheny Divide, and reached Huntingdon by 1850 and Duncansville in 1852 to provide a through link to Pittsburgh. The railroad was enormously successful. It hauled 70,000 tons of freight in its first year. The PRR expanded rapidly and built and acquired lines throughout the state. The through railroad that bypassed the incline portage sections was complete in 1854.

The character and heavily built infrastructure associated with the latter-day Pennsy was largely the result of early twentieth-century upgrades implemented by the railroad's president, Alexander John Cassatt. Under Cassatt, the railroad was expanded from two to four main tracks all the way to Pittsburgh.

The portion of the railroad between Harrisburg and Altoona was traditionally known as Middle Division and was located at the middle of the mainline between Philadelphia and Pittsburgh.

In its heyday, this route was a major freight and passenger corridor. It was best known for the *Broadway Limited* that raced between New York City and Chicago in competition with New York Central's *Twentieth Century Limited.* The line hosted dozens of other long-distance and local

Heading west on the former Pennsy Middle Division, this manifest blasts through Mexico, Pennsylvania, in May 1997. The train is led by one of Conrail's 135 EMD SD50s.
*Tim Doherty*

During the last weeks of Conrail, a Westward ballast train grinds through Thompsontown, Pennsylvania, on the old PRR Middle Division.
*Michael L. Gardner*

Conrail DASH 8-40CW 6163 rolls through Mapleton, Pennsylvania, on October 11, 1997. This route between Harrisburg and Altoona was traditionally part of PRR's famous Middle Division but under Conrail it was called the Pittsburgh Line. *Brian Solomon*

Following in the tradition Don Wood, who photographed of Pennsy's famous M1 Mountain-types racing along highway 22 east of Huntingdon, Pennsylvania, this photo of Conrail SD40-2 6467 was taken on July 27, 1987. *Brian Solomon*

Dozens of stored locomotives, largely early 1960s GP30s and GP35s that were poor performers with reliability problems, were captured on film in Altoona, Pennsylvania, on Easter Sunday 1988. *Brian Solomon*

passenger trains daily. By 1979, the route was reduced to one train, Amtrak's ragtag version of the *Broadway*. While this was later augmented by the New York–Pittsburgh *Pennsylvanian*, the railroad had primarily become a freight artery. Between 1985 and 1986, Conrail rebuilt the old Middle Division as a double-tracked railroad under CTC. This closed many towers along the line and transferred control of signals to Altoona. Most of the Victorian-era towers were bulldozed, but Hunt Tower in Huntingdon was preserved and is still maintained as a museum by a local group. Initially, Conrail retained PRR's classic position-light signal hardware, but the position light fell out of favor in the mid-1990s, and Conrail replaced them with its preferred triangular-patterned, color-light signal.

For many miles, the railroad closely follows the Juniata and crosses it repeatedly. This area was once filled with small industries and mines, and in PRR's heyday, the Middle Division served as a trunk route that connected numerous branches and secondary lines. By the late Conrail era, most

trackside industry along the Middle Division had left, branches had been chopped, and local traffic dwindled. A small yard and a junction with branches to Maitland and Milroy remains in Lewistown, and they were sold in 1996. These lines were transferred to Richard Robey, who also operates many former Conrail branches in central Pennsylvania. Farther west is Mount Union, a little-used junction where narrow gauge East Broad Top once interchanged coal and ore traffic with Pennsy. A little-used junction in Huntingdon is the last remnant of the Huntingdon & Broad Top Mountain coal-hauling line.

West of Huntington, the line turns northward and follows the Little Juniata River. It passes Warrior Ridge, the location of a Conrail automatic talking defect detector; and Petersburg, a former junction with a scenic branch to Hollidaysburg; and continues across the Barree Straight to the twin-bore Spruce Creek Tunnel. There are eight tortuous miles between the tunnel and Tyrone that keep train speeds to a moderate pace. Tyrone is a junction with the Bald

Eagle Branch that runs northeast to a junction with the Buffalo Line in Lock Haven. Conrail sold this dormant, tangent route to Robey's Nittany & Bald Eagle Railroad (N&BER) in the 1980s. With the help of a regional railway authority, N&BER reopened the line to through traffic and allowed Conrail (and later Norfolk Southern) coal trains to operate over the length of the line.

## ALTOONA

The city of Altoona is located at the base of the Allegheny Divide. The city owes its existence and prosperity to the Pennsylvania Railroad. The railroad's initial 1852 connection with the Main Line of Public Works was never more than a temporary solution for east-west traffic while Thomson surveyed and built his all-rail route across the Alleghenies. He selected the Horseshoe Curve Route so the railroad would be able to ascend nearly 1,000 feet in 12 miles, roughly equal to the entire climb accomplished in the more than 120 miles between Altoona and Harrisburg.

The Pennsylvania Railroad built an immense yard and shop complex in Altoona. PRR's Juniata Shops were more than a maintenance facility and eventually extended along more than 12 city blocks, covered 218 acres, and employed thousands of people. PRR built many of its most famous steam and electric locomotives at Juniata and was one of the largest producers of new steam locomotives.

Under Conrail, Juniata survived as the only heavy locomotive repair facility responsible for the entire Conrail fleet. In addition, Juniata provided heavy work for other railroads under contract. In 1994, Juniata resumed its traditional role as locomotive builder when it assembled new EMD SD60Ms for Conrail from kits supplied by the manufacturer.

In the Pennsy era, Altoona featured a sizeable classification yard complete with hump. Its primary function was to sort coal coming from the many mines on PRR's lines for eastward movements. As coal lines declined, so did the need for this yard. A portion of the yard remained to store surplus locomotives and freight cars.

Unlike many American cities, Altoona never lost its passenger services. By the late Conrail era, two pairs of daily Amtrak trains stopped for passengers at the passenger station near downtown.

## HORSESHOE CURVE

Railroaders have long referred to Pennsy's ascent of the Allegheny Divide as "The Mountain," as related by David P. Morgan in the April 1957 issue of *TRAINS Magazine*. Others know the whole grade as "The Curve." Either way, this is *the* big climb, not to be confused with any other mountain grade or horseshoe curve. This is tough railroading, and not every train makes it up or down the Mountain without incident. Conrail's Pittsburgh Division timetable had pages of special instructions dictating handling of eastward trains. One crucial paragraph reads: "If the brake pipe pressure on the controlling engine drops to 70 pounds from any cause, the train must be stopped and secured. Train must not proceed until brake pipe pressure has been restored."

If a train loses its air or doesn't have enough air as it descends the grade, an engineer may be unable to set the brakes sufficiently to keep the train in control. If control is lost, gravity takes over.

It is an awesome spectacle to watch a 600-axle train, helpers fore and aft, struggle to make the grade. Some trains do it in 45 minutes or less, and others can take well over an hour. The Mountain is tough not just because it was steep, curved, and heavily traveled, but because Conrail ran long westward and heavy eastward trains. These often needed help to ascend and descend the grade. Conrail assigned manned helpers to the Mountain. Five to eight helpers might

The roar of 20-cylinder, 645-series engines shatters the autumn air on October 21, 1979. A pair of SD45s shove Conrail ENIN (Enola Yard to Indianapolis) up the grade near Horseshoe Curve. Conrail often assigned older Electro-Motive six-motor power to helper service on its Pittsburgh Line. All of Conrail's Electro-Motive SD45s were retired or sold in the early 1980s, but its 13 former SD45-2s were retained and often assigned as helpers in the 1980s and 1990s. *Doug Eisele*

Conrail 6386, working as part of a two-unit head-end helper, leads an eastbound downgrade toward Altoona, Pennsylvania, at Slope on November 23, 1998. Conrail inherited the crossing of the Allegheny Divide from the Pennsylvania Railroad. This was the busiest mountain crossing in the United States. *Brian Solomon*

On July 7, 1990, B36-7 5003 leads GP40-2 3359 on westbound Mail 9H around Horseshoe Curve. Mail 9H is a Harrisburg to Chicago intermodal train that carries mail for the U.S. Postal Service and UPS. The several Conrail Mercury trailers behind the locomotives were Conrail's attempt at Premium Retail Intermodal transport. *Patrick Yough*

work between Altoona and Johnstown at any one time.

On the Mountain, many westward trains were helped from Altoona to Cresson. Others might keep helpers down the west slope to Johnstown to assist with braking, and some may be all the way to Pittsburgh. Likewise, eastward trains might take a helper at Johnstown, or farther west as required. However, through helpers were seldom used from Pittsburgh to Cresson. Cresson often based helpers down the grade east of Gallitzin. The whine of dynamic brakes indicates that the speed of a heavy train needs to be checked. The number of helpers and their placement varies depending on the size, weight, and makeup of a train. Intermodal trains often receive a head-end helper. Very heavy manifest trains may receive two or three helper sets (each with its own crew). Although rear-end placement is more typical, on rare occasions, helpers operate mid-train.

Thomson surveyed and supervised construction of the route west of Altoona toward Kittanning Point. Here the railroad loops into a splendid valley and makes its famous horseshoe-shaped bend to ascend a 1.85 percent ruling grade. Thomson's Allegheny mountain crossing was considered among the most significant engineering accomplishments of its time. Until the 1950s, Horseshoe Curve was often listed as one of the seven modern engineering wonders of the world. Pennsy built a park there in 1879, and often featured the Horseshoe Curve in promotions. The Curve has become a popular tourist destination, and a modern new visitors' center opened in 1992. The center is operated by the Railroaders Memorial Museum and allows the public to enjoy the never-ending parade of freight and passenger trains. In the early 1990s, more than 400,000 visitors came from around the world to view the Curve from the park.

## TUNNEL HILL

West of Horseshoe, the railroad follows Sugar Run Valley toward the summit. A mile and a half beyond the Curve is MG (mid-grade), the location of crossovers between all main tracks. The interlocking tower was built in 1944 and closed for regular use in 1978. Conrail occasionally reopened it in the 1980s during track work or when traffic was heavy. As the line approaches the summit, it negotiates Bennington Curve.

Pennsylvania Railroad used three tunnels beneath the Allegheny Divide. The two northern bores, Gallitzin and Allegheny Tunnels, are parallel, but the southernmost bore, the New Portage Tunnel, is on a different alignment and at a slightly higher elevation. The Gallitzin Tunnel was opened in 1904, and closed in the mid-1990s in conjunction with Conrail's clearance improvement project to allow double stacks across the Pittsburgh Division. Among other improvements to the route, clearances were raised in Allegheny and New Portage Tunnels, and the Allegheny Tunnel was enlarged for double track. The Gallitzin Tunnel has been retained as an access road, but could carry tracks in the future if traffic demands.

## MULE SHOE CURVE

The junction with the New Portage Secondary is east of the tunnels. This parallel crossing of the Alleghenies was originally graded in 1855 as a railway replacement for Portage Railway's inclined planes. It traversed the much-lesser-known Mule Shoe Curve, located several miles south of the Horseshoe. This improvement to the Main Line of Public Works was intended to help it compete with the recently completed PRR, but Pennsy bought the state-run transport system and abandoned the New Portage Railway Line within a year. Nearly five decades later, the track was re-layed to increase overall east-west route capacity and provide a slightly less steep (1.6 percent) but longer mountain crossing. It also provided a direct rail route between Hollidaysburg and Gallitzin. This line

The hazy morning sun glints off an eastward loaded coal train approaching the summit of the Alleghenies at Gallitzin at 7:06 a.m. on July 29, 1987. This image captures the spirit of the once-mighty Pennsylvania Railroad, the self-proclaimed standard railroad of the world. *Brian Solomon*

remained open until 1981, when Conrail abandoned it a second time.

### GALLITZIN

The village of Gallitzin straddles the hillside above the tunnels. To the west is a loop track between the two non-adjacent summit alignments that has been used to reverse helpers. Traditionally, the 60-lever AR tower controlled loop tracks, movements through the tunnels, and the junction with the New Portage Secondary. This Conrail tower, like most on the Mountain, was closed in the mid-1990s.

After cresting the Divide, the railroad descends for 27 miles to Johnstown. The ruling grade on the west slope is 1.25 percent for eastward trains, which is much less severe than the westward climb. Yet, eastward trains, especially loaded coal trains, are usually very heavy and make it a tough pull.

In its early years, the Mountain was double-track. By 1900, it had been expanded to four tracks. In the later Conrail period, it operated a continuous three-track mainline between Altoona and CONPIT Junction west of Johnstown. The modern arrangement uses the center track for bidirectional movements, and outside tracks for directional movements in the current of traffic. At choke points, additional tracks are maintained to relieve congestion and cut helpers on and off trains.

## CRESSON AND COAL BRANCHES

The PRR and Conrail based their helpers at Cresson, a small community on the west slope at milepost 251. The interlocking was controlled by MO tower, later CP MO after the tower was closed and unintentionally demolished while Conrail tried to move it for preservation. The modest engine terminal fuels the helper fleet and locomotives that work trains on coal branches northward from Cresson toward Clearfield and Keating, and to mines on the Irvona Secondary.

Pennsylvania coal had declined since World War II, and while coal branches north of Cresson lines remained moderately busy with coal traffic through the early 1990s, traffic was largely high-sulfur bituminous coal, which declined after the Clear Air Act passed in 1990. These coal branches were a mix of PRR and New York Central routes. In the 1990s, they were grouped by Conrail as the Clearfield Cluster and centered around the former NYC coal hub at Clearfield. It was sold to

The eastward loaded coal train, UFS 200, leaves Clearfield yard for Pennsylvania Power & Light's Montour Steam Electric Station near Washingtonville, Pennsylvania, at the end of the Watsontown secondary. A single crew handles the train from Clearfield to the power plant. A power pool consisting of 10 SD40-2's (6399-6410 less 6407) and 25 GP38-2's (8040-8064) were used to power these trains. The snowplows were later trimmed to clear the car dumper at Montour. Conrail sold the Clearfield Cluster to RJ Corman Pennsylvania Lines in December 1995. *Mark Leppert*

A stone arch carrying a connection to the Cresson Secondary branch frames Conrail SD40-2 6375 in Cresson, Pennsylvania, on October 17, 1992. Conrail's Irvona Branch and Cresson Secondary diverged at Cresson. Both lines were primary used by coal trains. *Brian Solomon*

R. J. Corman, a shortline operator, on December 31, 1995.

### LILLY, CASSANDRA TO SOUTH FORK, JOHNSTOWN, AND BEYOND

Descending past Cresson and Lilly, the Pittsburgh Line crosses the original Portage railway and the earlier alignments between Cassandra and Portage.

South Fork, Pennsylvania, is famous for the poorly constructed dam east of town that caused the famous Johnstown Flood of 1889. Legend has it that a wall of water raced down the valley, preceded by a locomotive with its whistle screaming to warn of the impending disaster. The flood wiped out the railroad along South Fork, as well as most of Johnstown.

Heavy snow in the Allegheny Mountains during the winter of 1992 disrupted service. To keep the railroad open, Conrail dispatched a snowplow extra SNO-201 using a Jordan spreader Cresson and South Fork. It plows eastbound on track number one at Summerhill on March 15, 1992. *Mark Leppert*

118

The village of South Fork is perched on the side of the hill above the railroad. Here, there is a junction, wye, and a yard. The South Fork Secondary diverges and ascends to the mines in Central City.

Situated in narrow river valleys, Johnstown evolved as a steel-making center in the years prior to the great flood. For most of the twentieth century, massive steelworks lined both sides of the Conemaugh River. Bethlehem Steel and Johnstown America built freight cars, including aluminum coal hoppers owned by electric utilities.

In Johnstown, C Tower controlled the interlockings on both sides of the city. At CONPIT Junction, 15 miles west of Johnstown, the mainlines split. Track Nos. 1 and 2 follow the south bank of the

Pennsylvania Railroad's characteristic position light signals were invented by Arthur Holley Rudd. He developed them during the World War I era, and they were primarily installed by PRR and its affiliates, Long Island Rail Road and Norfolk & Western. Although Conrail maintained PRR position lights, they were replaced with color-light signals in the mid-1990s. A westbound intermodal train rolls westward through South Fork, Pennsylvania, on October 17, 1992. *Brian Solomon*

Conrail local WISF-04 crossed Paint Creek at Scalp Level on the South Fork Secondary with empty hoppers enroute to the mines for loading. *Mark Leppert*

Conemaugh River, and track No. 3, known as the Sang Hollow extension, follows the north bank.

CP CONPIT, at milepost 290, is the junction with the Conemaugh Line. This alternate route was another of Cassatt's improvements. It runs parallel to the Pittsburgh Line and provides a 77-mile water level route to Pittsburgh. It features a gentler and significantly longer route for heavy freight. In the late 1980s, the Conemaugh Line was reduced to local traffic since it was a single track. In 1994, Conrail ran heavy eastbounds, such as PIOI (Conway to Oak Island) and coal trains, to avoid using helpers. The Pittsburgh Line continues west via Latrobe and crosses a series of low summits before it reaches its namesake. The massive steel complexes in Pittsburgh were largely silenced during industrial shifts in the early 1980s and provided limited traffic for Conrail. Pennsy's massive Pitcairn Yard closed in 1979. In the 1990s, Conrail constructed a completely new, thoroughly modern intermodal facility at Pitcairn for $9 million.

Reincarnated, Pitcairn captured the essence of Conrail's success. For more than a decade, its twisted, rusting rails and unused coal hoppers symbolized the collapse of heavy industry. Conrail observers, habitual naysayers, and industry pundits were amazed when railroads in the Northeast began to prosper after years of decay and contraction.

## FORT WAYNE LINE: PITTSBURGH TO CONWAY

Under Conrail, the divide between the Pittsburgh and Fort Wayne Lines was in downtown Pittsburgh at CP WEST PITT. Traditionally, the Fort Wayne Line was the primary PRR route to Chicago. In the L. Stanley Crane era, this changed as Chicago traffic was diverted west of Alliance, Ohio, to Cleveland, and then west via former New York Central routes. The Fort Wayne Line between Pittsburgh and Conway was typically the heaviest section of the Conrail system in terms of annual gross tons. Traffic was so intense that several sections of PRR's classic four-track mainline were retained despite rationalization and downsizing elsewhere.

## CONWAY YARD

Conway was important to the whole Conrail system. It was Conrail's largest yard, second only to Elkhart Yard. It measures four miles long, consists of 131 track miles, and features a double hump used to classify up to 3,500 cars daily. Built by PRR, the eastward classification yard opened to traffic in 1955, while the westward class yard opened two years later. Its vast size and exceptional high capacity permitted Conrail and its predecessors to close a host of smaller facilities locally and around the system. Most manifest freights worked Conway or used it as a terminal. In 1995, *TRAINS Magazine* reported that between 35 and 40 trains originated at Conway.

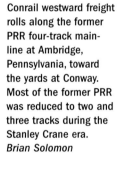

On July 26, 1987, a Conrail westward freight rolls along the former PRR four-track mainline at Ambridge, Pennsylvania, toward the yards at Conway. Most of the former PRR was reduced to two and three tracks during the Stanley Crane era. *Brian Solomon*

# MONONGAHELA RAILWAY

## *Patrick Yough*

Monongahela Railway (MGA) was the seventh largest coal hauler in the United States before integration into Conrail's Pittsburgh Division in the early 1990s. The Monongahela was originally owned equally by Baltimore & Ohio, Pennsylvania Railroad, and Pittsburgh & Lake Erie (New York Central). It was formed as a truce between the competing lines, which all wished to control movements from the rich coal reserves in far southwestern Pennsylvania.

B&O (later CSXT) had been a silent partner for many years. Much of the coal was destined to markets served by either PRR or P&LE. Ownership of the railroad changed in steps. First P&LE, suffering financially, sold to Conrail on December 26, 1989. Then CSXT sold its stake in the line to Conrail in March 1990.

A loaded coal train enroute from Consol's Bailey Mine in Time, Pennsylvania, on the Manor branch on October 22, 1992. The Manor branch was built by the Monongahela Railway in 1984 to tap a new coal mine built by Consol Energy. This train features old 70- and 100-ton hoppers that were rebuilt into rotary gondolas at Conrail's Samuel Rea Car Shops in Hollidaysburg. Mark Leppert

With the Monongahela purchase, Conrail assumed control of five of the largest deep bituminous coal mines east of the Mississippi. The most productive are Consol Energy's (formerly Consolidation Coal) Bailey and Enlow Fork mines. These, along with the Bailey Central Prep Plant, now produce approximately 20 million tons of coal annually. (By comparison, in 1989, Monongahela moved only 17 million tons of coal from all mines on its system; Enlow Fork did not come on line until 1990.) The Pittsburgh seam mines along the Monongahela Railway produce very valuable coal for contemporary markets.

Coal from these mines averages around 13,000 British thermal units per pound compared with just 9,000 British thermal units per pound for Wyoming Power River Basin coal. A high British thermal unit rate means the coal has more energy potential, and more significantly, it has comparatively low sulfur content.

## Thinking Ahead

In the mid-1980s, the traditional central Pennsylvania coal industry was dying. If Conrail wanted to keep hauling coal, it needed to examine Monongahela Railway's (MGA) traffic more closely. Most mines on MGA were relatively modern with high-capacity, load-in-motion balloon loops that filled unit trains in a few hours. On the MGA west division, six-axle locomotives could be used to load and deliver the trains to the power plants and docks. In contrast, typical central Pennsylvania mines did not have such arrangements and used front-end bucket loaders to fill coal hoppers that required crews to move each car forward after loading.

Another cost consideration was that central Pennsylvania unit coal trains required as many as nine four-axle locomotives because six-axle units were restricted on most branches. Extra crew and mechanical costs were required to place six-axle units on the train to forward it to the destination. Mining economics favored the MGA-origin mines since central Pennsylvania pits were either small strip mines or small, thin-seam underground mines. The deep mines were not suitable for modern longwall mining methods.

MGA-origin mines were ideally suited for longwall mining because their high seam heights made longwall mining more cost competitive. In January 1990, Conrail sold the Low Grade secondary and Lawsonham running track to the Mountain Laurel railroad.

In December 1995, Conrail sold its central Pennsylvania coal branches as the Clearfield Cluster to R. J. Corman Railroad Group. This included all branches north of Cresson, including the Irvona secondary, to Keating, Pennsylvania.

## Coal by Wire

In the mid-1960s, Pennsylvania Electric (Penelec) coined the phrase "Coal by Wire." Penelec built power plants in central and western Pennsylvania near coal reserves and produced electricity cheaper than on the East Coast. Energy could be more economically shipped via high-voltage transmission lines than by moving coal by rail. Penelec teamed up with several mining companies, including North American Coal Company (NACCO) and Rochester & Pittsburgh Coal, to build several large generating stations close to the coal mines. Mine-mouth plants have little or no coal transport costs. The most economical plant to operate on the PJM power grid was Conemaugh Station, located right in Huff near CONPIT Junction. Conemaugh's coal came from a conveyor belt from the Florence Mining Company preparation plant and was delivered from local strip mines by truck. When production problems began at Florence in the mid-1980s, Conrail had the opportunity to demonstrate its service. Originally Conrail leased a conveyor train designed and patented by the Georgetown railroad that operated in a circuit between Conemaugh Station and the Jubilee mine near Derry.

## Impact of the Clean Air Act of 1990

President George H. W. Bush signed a major revision to the Clean Air Act in 1990. This was aimed to stop acid rain caused by power plants that burned high-sulfur coal. This law was a major blow to small, independent coal producers in central Pennsylvania.

The Environmental Protection Agency (EPA) set up a program to install Continuous Emissions

Monitoring Systems (CEMS) in utility boilers to measure sulfur dioxide ($SO_2$) output, and issued fixed annual allowances based on $SO_2$ emissions. This let allowances be traded on the open market as needed. The first phase of the Clean Air Act targeted the "Big Dirties"—plants that generated the most $SO_2$. They were primarily in Pennsylvania, Ohio, Indiana, Illinois, West Virginia, and Maryland.

Conrail and the MGA-origin mines teamed up to market lower-sulfur coal from the Pittsburgh seam to power plants in Keystone, Conemaugh, Brunner Island, Montour, Chalk Point, Indian River, Dunkirk, and Eddystone. By burning lower-sulfur coal, plants could avoid installing costly Flue Gas Desulfurization (FGD) systems to remove $SO_2$ from the exhaust gas stream.

The two most cost effective plants in the PJM grid were the Keystone and Conemaugh Stations. A consortium of mid-Atlantic power companies owns Keystone and Conemaugh, and Pennsylvania Electric (Penelec) is the operator. Some utilities, including Penelec, added a wet limestone FGD system so Conemaugh could burn local high-sulfur coal and offset the costs of the FGD system. Conrail benefited from the increase of rail-hauled coal into Conemaugh from local high-sulfur mines in the Johnstown area, which was later augmented by coal from MGA-area mines.

While Penelec selected the FGD system for Conemaugh, it chose a different compliance strategy at its Keystone station. In 1994, Keystone started to sample coal from MGA mines delivered by Conrail via a circuitous route that included Pittsburg & Shawmut and Buffalo & Pittsburgh. To move coal from Cloe, Pennsylvania, on the B&P, Conrail purchased CSX's Indiana and Ridge subdivisions.

In September 1998, Consol increased Keystone's reliance on MGA coal by buying the Rochester & Pittsburgh Coal Company. On November 29, 1999, Consol closed the three mine-mouth plants that fed Keystone and renegotiated the coal supply contract to utilize the Bailey and Enlow Fork mines. Coal from the Bailey complex could be produced for about $8 a ton versus $23 from R&P's Indiana County mines.

*Monongahela Railway UGP 7, led by P&LE's former Conrail GP38, traverses street trackage in West Brownsville, Pennsylvania, on March 28, 1989. This train is enroute to be loaded at Eastern Associated Coal's Federal # 2 mine near Fairview, West Virginia. After it is loaded, it will go to the Glassport Transportation Center along P&LE's Mon Branch to be transloaded into barges for shipment to power plants.* Patrick Yough

# CHAPTER EIGHT

# CONRAIL LINES WEST
## *Conduits of Commerce*

Conrail's western lines were its vital arteries to funnel traffic to western connections and serve on-line industries. Historically, Conrail's predecessors operated dense and competitive midwestern networks. Conrail's ability to concentrate traffic onto a handful of midwestern routes was testimony to its successful rehabilitation of the bankrupt Penn Central network.

Conrail's Lines West covers routes in Ohio, Indiana, Illinois, West Virginia, and Michigan. These lines were under control of Pittsburgh, Dearborn, and Indianapolis Divisions after the administrative consolidations in 1988 and 1989. Lines West was a Pennsy term for its lines west of Pittsburgh. Despite the importance of these lines, they generally received less attention from the railroad and its chroniclers who focused on eastern routes and operations. Under Conrail control,

On the evening of January 9, 1994, SD40-2 6459 leads an eastward double stack in Elkhart, Indiana. Conrail's primary yard for Chicago traffic was the former New York Central facility in Elkhart. Here, trains were pre-blocked for Chicago-area connections. Movements, such as this doublestack, avoided the yard and operated via the mainline. *Brian Solomon*

Conrail's PRR heritage in the Midwest was gradually eradicated. Indianapolis blasted this relic to make way for Conseco Fieldhouse, the home of the Indiana Pacers. *Eric Powell*

former Pennsy Lines West fared badly. By 1999, except for the Fort Wayne Line across Ohio, very little of PRR's once vast and intensive route structure across the Midwest remained. Even the Fort Wayne Route had most of its traffic diverted. Conrail focused the majority of through traffic to former New York Central routes.

Midwestern operations were once characterized by numerous double- and multiple-track lines with frequent grade level crossings controlled by traditional interlocking towers. A web of Conrail branchlines connected towns across Ohio, Indiana, and Illinois. This picture changed during Conrail's tenure. Traditional directional double-track routes were converted to single-track CTC, usually in conjunction with resignaling. These projects closed most of the remaining towers and stripped lines of their predecessors' character.

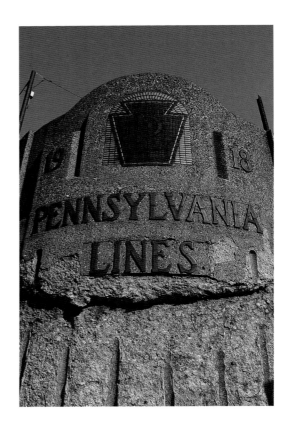

## NEW YORK CENTRAL LINES
## DEARBORN DIVISION

Conrail's Dearborn Division served the industrial heart of the rust belt with mostly

former New York Central lines. The region's remaining heavy industries generated significant Conrail traffic.

Conrail SD50 6727 leads a mixed freight west of Buffalo, New York, at Tifft Street on December 3, 1988. This view looks towards CP Draw and the junction with the Compromise Branch. A second westward train can be seen in the distance. Conrail maintained two routes through downtown Buffalo to accommodate a heavy volume of local and through freights. *Brian Solomon*

## CHICAGO LINE

The most significant route in the whole region was Conrail's Chicago Line that linked East Coast markets with the Chicago gateway—the largest freight interchange in the United States. The Chicago Line was the former New York Central mainline and was once largely four tracks all the way to Chicago. Under Conrail, this was operated primarily as double-track CTC with dispatcher-controlled passing sidings and short-sections of multiple-track CTC at busy locations.

West of Buffalo, the Chicago Line follows the shore of Lake Erie. This low-grade mainline raceway saw upwards of 50 trains daily in the later Conrail period. In Erie, Pennsylvania, the line passes General Electric's primary locomotive works that manufactured thousands of diesel-electric locomotives. New locomotives painted for many railroads were delivered by Conrail or trains working on the Chicago Line.

Conrail's Youngstown Line crossed at grade in Ashtabula, Ohio. This route was a north-south funnel that connected coal and ore docks with steel works and coal mines farther south. As many as 10 loaded and empty mineral trains traveled the line

Conrail BUTO (Buffalo, New York, to Toledo, Ohio) works Seneca Yard, near CP5, in Blasdell, New York, on May 21, 1989. Conrail inherited three overhead bridges at this location from its various predecessors. The most distant bridge pictured here is the former Lehigh Valley freight main. The next is the former PRR route known as the Ebenezer secondary that connected with the Buffalo Line, and the closest was the former New York Central Gardenville Branch. The Ebenezer Secondary was the only active bridge during the Conrail–era. The other bridges were removed in the 1990s. *Brian Solomon*

daily along with other traffic from former PRR territories.

Cleveland served as an important junction on New York Central Lines. New York Central located a large classification yard and primary heavy locomotive shops in Collinwood. Until the early 1990s, massive Hulett unloaders were used to transfer iron ore from lake ships to trains at Cleveland's Whiskey Island Docks.

Berea, west of Cleveland, is a major junction. Traditionally Berea Tower controlled crucial junctions with Conrail's Indianapolis Line and its Cleveland Short Line Branch. Berea is the center of Conrail's huge "X," which made it one of the busiest places on the system. Berea's interlocking plant dated from New York Central times, and the tower lasted to near the end of the Conrail era. It closed in February 1998,

when its functions were transferred to a dispatcher's desk in Dearborn, Michigan.

Most of the way between Buffalo and Toledo, the Chicago Line runs parallel with the Lake Erie shoreline. The tracks are very near the water at Sandusky Bay where they cross it on the Bay Bridge. High winds have blown intermodal trailers off passing trains in Sandusky.

The Detroit Line was Conrail's former New York Central north-south route and connected Toledo with its namesake. Under Conrail, this was a primary artery that served auto plants in northern Ohio and southern Michigan. This was one of the few heavily used Conrail lines remaining in Michigan. Pennsy's Detroit line, known as the Lincoln Secondary under Conrail, was primarily used for local traffic, although the line was going to be upgraded in conjunction with the

CSX/NS split. New York Central and PRR had once operated extensive lines throughout Michigan, but most had been rationalized during Penn Central and the early Conrail era. Detroit generated considerable traffic for Conrail, and several important yards operated there, including River Rouge, North Yard, and Livernois.

A few miles east of Elkhart, near Goshen, Indiana, is a junction with a north-south route that extended 113 miles to South Anderson, Indiana. In the later days of Conrail, it was known as the Marion Branch and served as a link for traffic that moved from northern Ohio and Michigan points to the St. Louis Line. It was Conrail's westernmost north-south connection. PRR and NYC maintained a host of north-south

routes in Indiana and Illinois at one time, but all were severed by the 1990s.

## CHICAGO AREA

Conrail's primary yard that handled traffic moving through the Chicago gateway was in Elkhart, Indiana, 100 miles east of Chicago. Elkhart was a vast freight hub that dated from the New York Central era that classified traffic from all across the system. Trains were made up for Chicago-area connections at Elkhart. The Chicago Line between Elkhart and Chicago was one of the busiest on the Conrail system in the number of trains moved. Dozens of through trains ran directly from Elkhart to Chicago. Inbound trains often operated with run-through motive power. Between Elkhart and

Conrail moved coal and ore via its docks on Lake Erie in Ashtabula, Ohio. In the mid-1990s, Conrail renumbered some SD40/SD40-2 out of the 6000 series to make room for new GE six-motor units. Conrail 0808 is seen in Ashtabula, amidst mountains of iron ore on October 23, 1994. *Brian Solomon*

Chicago, interchange trains often ran with Burlington Northern, Chicago & North Western, Santa Fe, Union Pacific, or other off-line locomotives. Symbol freights reflected the origin/destination of interchange trains: ELPR/PREL operated between Elkhart and C&NW's Proviso Yard; ELIC/ICEL to Illinois Central's Riverdale Yard; and ELBN/BNEL to Burlington Northern's Cicero Yard. In addition to manifest (carload traffic) was Conrail's parade of priority inter-modal trains. Some of this traffic terminated in Chicago, primarily at the intermodal facilities at 51st and 55th Streets. Other trains were interchanged with western lines, such as TVLA's joint operation with Santa Fe. This coast-to-coast speedster connected the New York metro area and Los Angeles on a tightly scheduled three-day run. American President Lines' double stacks moved from West Coast ports to Conrail via C&NW. Automobile traffic in unit multilevel trains was also a key traffic component on this route.

The Chicago Line passed massive steel-making complexes near Gary, Indiana. These plants stretch for miles and provide steel for auto plants around Detroit.

*Above:* An eastward freight on the Chicago Line, lead by C36-7 6629, crosses the Maumee River in Toledo, Ohio. The region between Toledo and Detroit has many auto manufacturing plants and was a significant source of Conrail traffic. *Peter Ruesch*

*Right:* New York Central's Water Level Route crossed Sandusky Bay on a long fill near Bayview, Ohio. A morning eastbound, led by a General Electric DASH 8-40CW, rolls toward Bayview on April 5, 1998. T.S. Hoover.

130

In addition to Elkhart, Conrail routed carload traffic to Indiana Harbor Belt Yards at Gibson and Blue Island and Belt Railway of Chicago's Clearing Yard.

## STREATOR CONNECTION

The Conrail–Santa Fe interchange could avoid continual rail traffic congestion in Chicago by using the Streator Connection. Traditionally this was a circuitous route to Streator, Illinois, that used the former New York Central Wheatfield Branch across farmland in Indiana and Illinois to connect with the Chicago Line at South Bend, Indiana. The routing was later adjusted, using a combination of the Porter branch to the Indiana Harbor Belt's Hammond Yard, and then Kankakee Line to the Streator Secondary. This route was less direct, but it gave Conrail greater operational flexibility and avoided the bulk of Chicago's congestion. The line continued beyond Streator to a steel plant in Hennepin, Illinois. Traffic on this route fluctuated as it came in and out of favor over the years. Toward the end of Conrail, *CTC Board* reported that operations included of a pair of through-interchange trains between Elkhart and Santa Fe's Kansas City Yard (ELSF/SFEL), Elkhart to Kankakee (ELKA/KAEL), and steel trains to Hennepin from the Cleveland area. In addition, there were local freights and unit coal trains that traveled to the power plant on the Wheatfield Line.

## BIG FOUR

Conrail's east-west traffic divided at Berea. Here, the Indianapolis Line, which handled through traffic toward Indianapolis and St. Louis, left from the Chicago Line.

Conrail's Indianapolis Line was the mainline of New York Central subsidiary, known as the Big Four (the Cleveland, Cincinnati, Chicago & St. Louis Railway Company). In the steam era, the Big Four operated more than 2,300 route miles to connect its namesake cities. The busy

double-track to Indianapolis via St. Louis hosted many famous New York Central passenger trains including the New York–St. Louis *Southwestern Limited*. Conrail converted the section between Berea to Crestline, Ohio, to single-track CTC in 1982. In anticipation of the split between CSX and NS, Conrail reinstalled the second main track to make the line double-track

One of Conrail's largest yards to organize traffic moving via the Chicago gateway was in Elkhart, Indiana, roughly 100 miles east of Chicago. *Peter Ruesch*

During the Stanley Crane era, Conrail focused all Chicago-bound traffic on New York Central's Water Level Route, which left the former PRR Fort Wayne Line devoid of through traffic. After Amtrak vacated the Fort Wayne Line in 1990, the west end of the route was severed and sold to Norfolk Southern. In contrast, the New York Central line between Cleveland and Chicago often accommodated 80 freights or more daily. Conrail 5640 leads a westward freight west of South Bend, Indiana, on Halloween. *Brian Solomon*

By July 1996, the operator at Bend tower in South Bend, Indiana, works on borrowed time as crews worked to complete the reconfiguration of the Grand Truck Western and Conrail crossing. Prior to reconfiguration, GTW trains had to use more than two miles of joint trackage. GTW trains were limited to one move at time. The new arrangement allowed the Conrail Chicago East Dispatcher to move two GTW trains simultaneously through the Conrail plant on a short section of shared trackage. Peter Ruesch

Working against a backdrop of the Chicago Skyline, a pair of Conrail DASH 8-40CWs, led by 6196, bring interchange traffic to Burlington Northern's Cicero Yard at Halsted Avenue, on March 4, 1995. *Brian Solomon*

CTC. In Crestline, the Big Four route crossed the former PRR Fort Wayne Line. East-west traffic moved over the Fort Wayne Route from Conway Yard, and points east joined the Indianapolis Line here. In Galion, five miles west of Crestline, the Columbus Line diverged from the Indianapolis Line and formed a component to the route that linked cities in southwestern Ohio.

Columbus was a crossroads for Conrail operations in Ohio and the location of Buckeye Yard. The city served as a major warehouse and distribution center for central Ohio. Clothing retailer The Limited operated its national distribution center in northeastern Columbus and shipped its products by Conrail intermodal services.

The Cincinnati Line traverses 117 miles to and from Columbus via Dayton and its namesake. This provided Conrail with important Norfolk Southern and CSX connections via the Cincinnati gateway. The route primarily accommodated mixed carload freight and auto traffic destined for interchange. When Conrail assumed operations, this route was traditional directional double-track. Operations were modernized in 1990 and 1991. Conrail installed a CTC system that reduced the route to single track, closed manned interlocking towers, and moved operations to the Indianapolis Division dispatcher's office in Indianapolis.

Conrail operated another former New York Central route southward from Columbus to Charleston, West Virginia. This line was used to haul coal. Manned helpers were assigned until Conrail initiated the use of unmanned remote control helpers, known as distributed power units. General Electric DASH 8-40Cs were equipped as head-end master units and mid-train slaves in the summer of 1994.

Conrail's Toledo Branch/*Scottlawn Secondary* was comprised of a north-south route that had been New York Central subsidiary Toledo & Ohio Central. In Conrail's later days, this was operated as a

single-track CTC line that connected Toledo and Columbus and had passing sidings every 10 miles.

## INDIANAPOLIS

In the 1988 reorganization, the Indianapolis Division was expanded to include the Columbus and Southwest Division. In conjunction with this change, train dispatchers in Columbus were relocated to Indianapolis, which served as a traditional hub with lines in all directions. During its 23-year tenure, Conrail closed and sold many lines that once connected Indianapolis with other midwestern cities, which left the Cleveland to St. Louis route via Indianapolis and St. Louis Lines as the most important line through the city. Lines, such as the former PRR route between Louisville and Indianapolis, were sold to shortline companies.

The largest facility in the region was the former New York Central Big Four Yard in Avon, Indiana, 10 miles west of Indianapolis on the St. Louis Line. According to Conrail, this hump yard featured 55 classification tracks, 11 receiving tracks, and departure tracks in 1983. At that time, it received 26 trains and sent out 30 trains daily, and processed an average of 1,578 cars daily. In 1991, Conrail downgraded the yard, closed the hump, and transferred classification work to Buckeye Yard in Columbus, Stanley Yard in Toledo, and other points around the system.

## ST. LOUIS LINE

Trains destined for the St. Louis gateway continued west of Indianapolis on the 237-mile-long St. Louis Line. This line that runs via Terre Haute blends the best sections of former New York Central and Pennsy routes between Indianapolis and East St. Louis. It angles south-west and crosses a variety of other lines at grade including CSX's line between Evansville, Indiana, and Danville, Illinois, at Terre Haute; a junction with Conrail's Danville Secondary that runs north-northwest toward Danville, Illinois; the north-south Illinois Central mainline in Effingham, Illinois; and the former Chicago and Eastern Illinois in St. Elmo, Illinois. Here Conrail and Union Pacific maintained an important interchange and exchange to

Chicago is America's foremost railroad city and features numerous complicated junctions, yards, and terminals. Brighton Park, on the former Alton route (later Illinois Central), was the junction of three lines: the former New York Central Chicago Junction, former Baltimore & Ohio Chicago Terminal, and the former Pennsylvania Railroad Panhandle route. This crossing was not interlocked, so all trains had to stop and wait to be flagged across with mechanical semaphores. On December 18, 1994, Conrail GP40-2 3373 passes Brighton Park, on the last leg of its westward journey.
*Brian Solomon*

***Below:*** The spring of 1978 was a time in Conrail history when there was still considerable reliance upon locomotives from Alco. CR component Erie Lackawanna essentially dictated the changes that delineated Century 424s and Century 425s and promptly purchased the new model, as did the NH. Here, two from the stable of NH, are fully repainted and leave the siding at Girard, Ohio, with an empty ore train.
*George S. Pitarys*

135

GP15-1s 1603 and 1607 lead Indianapolis Terminal local freight symbol IT-32 on the former Indianapolis Union Railway mainline, located south of downtown Indianapolis, on October 13, 1998. EMD GP15-1s were a 1,500 horsepower road-switcher type built in the 1970s with recycled components. They were found all across the Conrail system and were often used on Indianapolis area locals. *Eric Powell*

avoid the congestion in St. Louis.

## TUSCAN RED BLUES PANHANDLE LINE

Pennsylvania Railroad operated two through routes between Pittsburgh and Chicago. The southern route was the Pittsburgh, Cincinnati, Chicago & St. Louis, better known as the Panhandle. These routes lost traffic to lines prior to Conrail, but the Panhandle Route between Pittsburgh and Columbus accommodated 25 to 30 trains a day until it was downgraded in 1981. St. Louis-bound traffic that once traveled the

Panhandle was diverted via the Fort Wayne Line to Crestline, and then onto the Indianapolis Line toward St. Louis. For a decade, the Pittsburgh–Columbus portions of the Panhandle survived as a secondary track. Conrail sold the direct westward connection in Pittsburgh to a local transit authority. Much of the trackage between Pittsburgh and Mingo Junction was abandoned. In the early 1990s, the Ohio Central shortline network assumed operations of the line from a point west of Mingo Junction to Columbus.

In eastern Ohio, the former PRR Route

latter-day Pittsburgh–Chicago traffic, and continues to serve NS as part of its main east-west New York–Chicago corridor.

### FORT WAYNE LINE

The most important former PRR line west of Pittsburgh was the Fort Wayne Route. The Fort Wayne Route was preferred for traffic that moved between Pittsburgh and Chicago until Conrail shifted freight traffic via the Cleveland Line and former Water Level Route in the early 1980s. Virtually all Conrail Chicago traffic followed this route by 1984. Although Fort Wayne was much less important than in earlier times, it did not dry up entirely. West of Crestline, the route was lightly traveled beginning in the early 1980s. The line retained local traffic as far as Bucyrus, Ohio, and Amtrak traversed the line daily until 1990, when it shifted its *Capitol Limited* to a Chicago Line routing west of Cleveland. Amtrak was the glue that held the Fort Wayne together as a contiguous route. With Amtrak gone, Conrail decommissioned block signaling west of Bucyrus, and the west portion was essentially void of traffic. In addition, Conrail installed CTC on the Alliance to Crestline section and removed several sections of traditional directional

This former Pennsylvania Railroad position-light signal is seen in Dunkirk, Indiana. The position-light was developed by Arthur Holley Rudd, one of PRR's leading signal engineers and a world renowned signal engineer. The signal uses three lights to mimic upper-quadrant semaphore aspects. This style of position-light was introduced in 1921 and became PRR's standard signal hardware. *Peter Ruesch*

ran northward along the Ohio River Valley from Powhatan via Mingo Junction to Yellow Creek and survived as a conduit for mineral traffic. This line was known as the River Line, but should not be confused with the former West Shore route along the Hudson, which is also known as the River Line. The Cleveland Line was another significant former PRR line under Conrail that formed an alternate route to the Fort Wayne Route between Rochester, Pennsylvania, (railroad direction west) and Alliance, Ohio, and then northward to its namesake. The Alliance–Cleveland portion of this line was an integral link for Conrail's

It is 12 degrees Fahrenheit, as Conrail symbol freight TRIN (St. Louis/TRRA to Indianapolis) glides over a distinctive concrete arch bridge over White Lick Creek in Danville, Indiana, on December 9, 1995. This bridge is characteristic of the style used by New York Central subsidiary, the Big Four. *Eric Powell*

double track. Portions of the western Fort Wayne Route were reborn in 1993 when Norfolk Southern bought the Warsaw to Valparaiso, Indiana, section to provide relief to its heavily traveled former Nickel Plate Road lines. As the cooperative Norfolk Southern–Conrail RoadRailer traffic blossomed in 1994, Conrail operated RoadRailers via Fort Wayne, Indiana, to Crestline and east.

The westernmost portion of the Fort Wayne Route between Hammond, Indiana,

Eastward Conrail ASIN-1 (Alton & Southern/ St. Louis to Indianapolis) uses track No. 2 at Haley Tower in Terre Haute, Indiana. This tower controlled the junction of Conrail's St. Louis Line with CSX's Chicago–Evansville, the former Chicago & Eastern Illinois mainline. *Peter Ruesch*

and Chicago essentially ran parallel to the New York Central Water Level Route. Under Conrail, this portion of the PRR prevailed over the New York Central. In Hammond, the Chicago Line cut over from the NYC alignment to PRR's and followed it the rest of the way into Chicago.

The grades on the Fort Wayne Route required helpers in both directions. The whole Fort Wayne Line between Conway and

Crestline was a helper district. According to *CTC Board Railroads Illustrated*, Wooster Hill, located between Big Run and Orrville, Ohio, has a 0.88 percent ruling grade eastward. In the late Conrail era, helpers based in Canton, Ohio, typically consisted of a pair of four-axle locomotives and ran light westward to help a heavy eastward train. Through helpers based at Conway or Mingo Junction worked mineral trains headed west.

## AUTOMOBILE TRAFFIC

Automotive traffic was one of Conrail's most important traffic divisions. According to *Jane's World Railways*, Conrail moved 20 percent of all finished automotive vehicles in the United States and was the largest carrier of automotive parts in 1994. In that year, Conrail served 23 assembly plants and 59 automotive component factories. The largest concentration of automotive factories was in northern Ohio and southern Michigan. To handle finished automotive traffic, Conrail had a fleet of approximately 5,500 multilevel autoracks. *Jane's* indicates there were 2,900 trilevel and 2,600 bilevel racks. Conrail operated a network of tightly scheduled dedicated multilevel trains to deliver vehicles.

Loaded autoracks cannot be sorted at hump yards since the process risks damage to new cars, so loaded autoracks were flat-switched. In later years, Cleveland's Collinwood Yard was Conrail's primary eastward multilevel

hub. While empty westward autoracks were at Seneca Yard in Buffalo, Gibson Yard in Hammond, Indiana, served as a secondary hub for the Chicago area, needed largely for interchange with other lines. In the mid-1990s, Conrail assigned the ML designation to its dedicated multilevel trains. Prior to that, auto-carrying trains used the origin-destination alpha code system assigned to manifest carload freight.

To increase cooperation and better serve auto producers, Conrail and Norfolk Southern shifted the autorack interchange point to Cleveland in the 1990s to replace various interchanges in the Midwest. With this arrangement, once the loaded autorack cars arrived from NS served plants, trains will be made up to serve Conrail distribution terminals in Albany, New York; Framingham (Westboro) and Ayer Massachusetts; and Newark and Ridgefield Heights, New Jersey.

# BIBLIOGRAPHY

## Books

*1846-1896 Fiftieth Anniversary of the Incorporation of the Pennsylvania Railroad Company.* Philadelphia, 1896.

*All Stations: A Journey Through 150 years of Railway History.* Paris, 1978.

Allen, G. Freeman. *The Fastest Trains in the World.* London, 1978.

Bean, W.L. *Twenty Years of Electrical Operation on the New York, New Haven, and Hartford Railroad.* East Pittsburgh, Pennsylvania, 1927.

Bezilla, Michael. *Electric Traction on the Pennsylvania Railroad 1895-1968.* State College, Pennsylvania, 1981.

Brignano, Mary and Hax McCullough. *The Search for Safety.* American Standard New York, 1981.

Bruce, Alfred W. *The Steam Locomotive in America.* New York, 1952.

Burgess, George, H., and Miles C. Kennedy. *Centennial History of the Pennsylvania Railroad.* Philadelphia, 1949.

Bush, Donald J. *The Streamlined Decade.* New York, 1975.

Casey, Robert J. and W.A.S. Douglas. *The Lackawanna Story.* McGraw-Hill, New York, 1951.

Churella, Albert, J. *From Steam to Diesel.* Princeton, New Jersey, 1998

Condit, Carl. *Port of New York, Vols. 1 & 2.* Chicago, 1980, 1981.

Crane, L. Stanley. *Rise from the Wreckage: A Brief History of Conrail.* New York 1988

Cupper, Dan. *Horseshoe Heritage: The Story of a Great Railroad Landmark.* Halifax, Pennsylvania, 1996.

Daughen, Joseph R., and Peter Binzen. *The Wreck of the Penn Central.* Boston, 1971.

Diehl, Lorraine B. *The Late Great Pennsylvania Station.* New York, 1985

Dooley, Frank. *Railroad Law a Decade after Deregulation.* Westport, Connecticut, 1994

Droege, John A. *Freight Terminals and Trains.* New York, 1912.

Droege, John A. *Passenger Terminals and Trains.* New York, 1916.

Drury, George H. *The Historical Guide to North American Railroads.* Waukesha, Wisconsin, 1985.

Drury, George H. *Guide to North American Steam Locomotives.* Waukesha, Wisconsin, 1993.

Drury, George H. *New York Central in the Hudson River Valley.* Waukesha, Wisconsin, 1995

Ely, James W. *Railroads and American Law.* Lawrence, Kansas, 2001.

Farrington, Jr., S. Kip. *Railroads at War.* New York, 1944.

Farrington, Jr., S. Kip. *Railroading from the Rear End.* New York, 1946.

Farrington, Jr., S. Kip. *Railroads of Today.* New York, 1949

Fischler, Stan. *Next Stop Grand Central.* Erin, Ontario, 1986.

Grant, H. Roger. *Erie Lackawanna: Death of an American Railroad 1938-1992.* Stanford, California, 1994

Hager, James. *Conrail's Philadelphia Division.* Whitehouse Station, New Jersey, 1998.

Harlow, Alvin F. *Steelways of New England.* New York, 1946.

Harlow, Alvin F. *The Road of the Century.* New York, 1947.

Hartley, Scott. *Conrail Volumes 1&2.* Piscataway, New Jersey, 1990.

*History of General Railway Signal Company.* Rochester, New York, 1979.

Holton, James L. *Reading Railroad History of a Coal Age Empire Volume 2.* Laurys Station, Pennsylvania, 1992

Hungerford, Edward. *Men of Erie.* New York, 1946

Jones, Robert W. *Boston & Albany: The New York Central in New England, Vols. 1 & 2.* Los Angeles, 1997.

Karr, Ronald Dale. *The Rail Lines of Southern New England.* Pepperell, Massachusetts, 1995.

Kirkland, John, F. *Dawn of the Diesel Age.* Pasadena, California, 1994.

Klein, Aaron E. *The History of the New York Central System.* New York, 1985.

Marre, Louis A. and Jerry A. Pinkepank. *The Contemporary Diesel Spotter's Guide.* Milwaukee, Wisconsin, 1985.

Marre, Louis, A. *Diesel Locomotives: The First 50 Years.* Waukesha, Wisconsin, 1995.

Marshall, John. *The Guinness Book of Rail Facts and Feats.* Enfield, Middlesex, United Kingdom, 1975.

Middleton, William D. *When the Steam Railroads Electrified.* Milwaukee, Wisconsin, 1974.

Middleton, William D. *Grand Central . . . the World's*

*Greatest Railway Terminal.* San Marino, California, 1977.

Middleton, William D. *Manhattan Gateway: New York's Pennsylvania Station.* Waukesha, Wisconsin, 1996.

Middleton, William D. *Landmarks on the Iron Road.* Bloomington, Indiana, 1999.

Mulhearn, Daniel J. and John R. Taibi. *General Motors' F-Units.* New York, 1982.

Nowak, Ed. *Ed Nowak's New York Central.* Park Forest, Illinois. 1983.

Orenstein, Jeffrey R. *United States Railroad Policy: Uncle Sam at the Throttle,* Chicago, 1990.

Pawson, John R. *Delaware Valley Rails.* Willow Grove, Pennsylvania, 1979.

Potter, Janet Greenstein. *Great American Railroad Stations.* New York, 1996.

Protheroe, Ernest. *The Railways of the World.* London.. 1914

Reiser, Hal. *Bridge Line Blues: Delaware & Hudson 1976-1986.* Glendale, California, 1989

Salsbury, Stephen. *No Way to Run a Railroad,* New York, 1982.

Smith, Warren L. *Berkshire Days on the Boston & Albany.* New York, 1982.

Snell, J. B. *Early Railways.* London, 1972.

Solomon, Brian. *The American Steam Locomotive.* Osceola, Wisconsin, 1998.

Solomon, Brian. *Railroad Stations.* New York, 1998

Solomon, Brian and Mike Schafer. *New York Central Railroad.* Osceola, Wisconsin, 1999.

Staufer, Alvin F. *Pennsy Power III.* Medina, Ohio, 1993.

Staufer, Alvin F. *Steam Power of the New York Central System, Volume 1.* Medina, Ohio, 1961

Staufer, Alvin F. and Edward L. May. *New York Central's Later Power.* Medina, Ohio, 1981

Steinman, David B. and Sara Ruth Watson. *Bridges and Their Builders.* New York, 1957.

Stevens, Frank W. *The Beginnings of the New York Central Railroad.* New York, 1926.

Stilgoe, John R. *Metropolitan Corridor.* New Haven, Connecticut, 1983.

Taber, Thomas Townsend, III. *The Delaware, Lackawanna & Western Railroad: Part One.* Williamsport, Pennsylvania. 1980.

Talbot, F. A. *Railway Wonders of the World, Volumes 1 & 2.* London, 1914.

Thompson, Slason. *Short History of American Railways.* Chicago, 1925.

Trewman, H.F. *Electrifcation of Railways.* London, 1920.

U.S. Department of Transportation. *Northeastern Railroad Problem: A report to the Congress.* Washington, D.C., 1973

United States Railway Association. *Preliminary System Plan Volume 1&2.* Washington, D.C., 1975

United States Railway Association. *Final System Plan Volume 1&2.* Washington, D.C., 1975

United States Railway Association. *Federal funding of Conrail: rail service objectives and economic realities.* Washington, D.C., 1980

Westing, Frederic. *Penn Station: Its Tunnels and Side Rodders.* Seattle, 1977.

Williams, Gerry. *Trains, Trolleys & Transit, A Guide to Philadelphia Area Rail Transit.* Piscataway, New Jersey, 1998.

Wilner, Frank N. *Railroad Mergers: History, Analysis, Insight.* Omaha, Nebraska, 1997.

Winchester, Clarence. *Railway Wonders of the World, Volumes 1 & 2.* London, 1935.

Zimmermann, Karl R. *Erie Lackawanna East.* New York, 1975.

Zimmermann, Karl R. *The Remarkable GG1.* New York, 1977.

## Periodicals

*Baldwin Locomotives.* Philadelphia, Pennsylvania.

*CTC Board—Railroads Illustrated.* Ferndale, Washington.

*Conrail Inside Track.* Philadelphia, Pennsylvania.

*Diesel Era,* Halifax, Pennsylvania.

*Jane's World Railways.* London.

*Locomotive & Railway Preservation.* Waukesha, Wisconsin.

*Mass Transit.* Fort Atkinson, Wisconsin.

*Modern Railroads.* New York

*Official Guide to the Railways.* New York

*RailNews.* Waukesha, Wisconsin.

*Railpace.* Piscataway, New Jersey.

*Railroad History,* formerly *Railway and Locomotive Historical Society Bulletin.* Boston, Massachusetts.

*Rails Northeast.* East McKeesport, Pennsylvania.

*Railway Age,* Chicago and New York.

*Railway Gazette, 1870-1908,* New York.

*The Railway Gazette,* London.

*Trains Magazine.* Waukesha, Wisconsin.

*Vintage Rails.* Waukesha, Wisconsin.

*Washington Post.* Washington, D.C.

## Other Sources

Association of American Railroads. *American Railway Signaling Principles and Practices.* New York, 1937.

Conrail. Annual Reports 1976-1998.

Conrail, Division Timetables.

Conrail *Form 10-K,* accessed thru EDGAR www.sec.gov.

Conrail. *Freight Schedules.*

Conrail, Office of Chief Engineer. *Maps and Traffic Density Charts.*

Conrail, *Options for Conrail, Conrail's Response to Section 703[c] of the Staggers Rail Act of 1980 (Executive Summary),*1981.

General Code of Operating Rules, Fourth Edition. 2000.

General Electric. *Dash 8 Locomotive Line.*

General Electric. *GE Locomotives.*

General Railway Signal. *Centralized Traffic Control, Type H, Class M, Coded System, Handbook 20.* Rochester, New York, 1941.

Metro-North Railroad, *Rules of the Operating Department*, 1999.

Metro-North Railroad, *Timetable No. 1.* 2001.

New York Central System. *Rules for the Government of the Operating Department.* 1937

New York and Long Branch Railroad. *Automatic Block and Interlocking Signals.* Printed 1906, reprinted 1975.

NORAC Operating Rules, 7th Edition. 2000

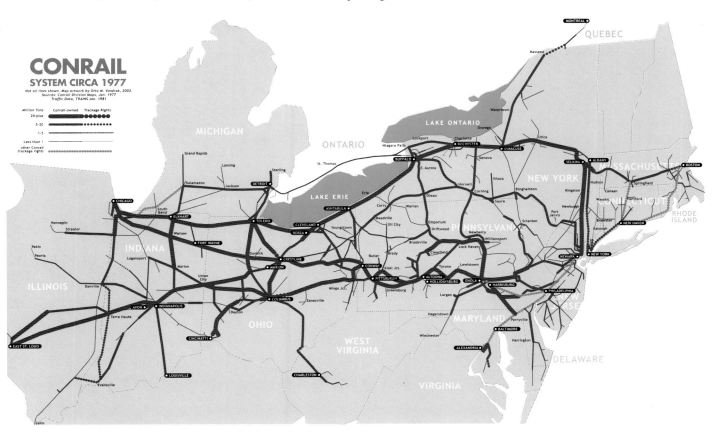

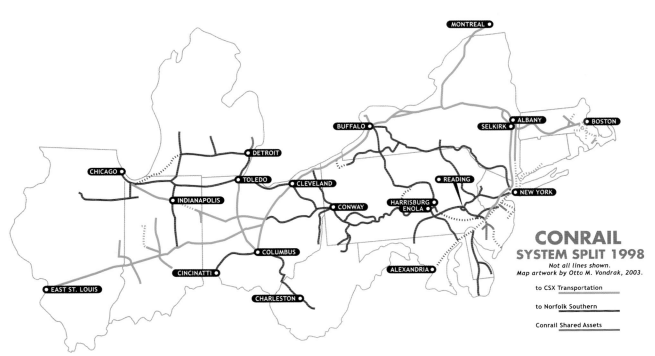

# INDEX